The

Sixth Star

text by Mae Silver

images by Sue Cazaly

This book is dedicated to the thousands of women who spent their
lives in pursuit of the women's vote in California. . .

The Sixth Star.

The Sixth Star

★ ★ ★ ★ ★ ★

West Coast suffragists crafted a flag with a star
symbolizing the suffrage states of Wyoming,
Colorado, Utah, Idaho and Washington. In 1911,
when California women won their right to vote,
California became the Sixth Star in the suffragist banner.

The collection is in five parts:

Acknowledgments

The material used in this collection of California women's political history came from the Bancroft Library, Berkeley; the California Historical Society, San Francisco; the California State Library, Sacramento; and the San Francisco Main Library. We wish to thank every single member of the staffs of these great houses of San Francisco archives. Especially, we thank these members of the History Center of the San Francisco Main: Susan Goldstein, archivist, Pat Akre, Selby Collins, Stan Carroll, Tom Carey, Christina Morietta, Thos Fowler, Faun McInnis, Susie Taylor, and Andrea Grimes, who behaved not only as research assistants, but as cheerleaders. They supported us through the challenging times we spent shaping this unique collection. We thank Dr. Lynn Bonfield and Susan Sherwood of the Labor Archives and Research Center and Dr. Sue Englander for their ideas and direction.

On a separate note, we wish to thank Chris Carlsson, who caught the spirit of *The Sixth Star* and truly helped it rise on every page.

Many thanks to typist Susan Pedrick, Glenn Caley Bachmann and editor Rhona Simmons for their invaluable help in shaping the writing of this book.

Our appreciation also goes to Donald Felton for his collaboration with Sue in creating a slideshow from this collection and refining images for the collection in the book.

This collection of California women's political history is a California first. To this date, no one else has produced such an exhibition in the form of a book. At times we found some women's photographs without captions and did our best to put names in place. That, too, was historic! Our hope is to see this material used by students in this state where women should feel proud about the legacy of their political predecessors. You, the reader, have no need to leave your comfortable reading chair to find this women's political history. In the year 2000, we present *The Sixth Star* to you with pleasure and joy.

Mae Silver and
Sue Cazaly

The
Sixth
Star

text by Mae Silver

images by Sue Cazaly

PUBLISHED BY
Ord Street Press
71 Ord Street
San Francisco, CA 94114

ISBN 0-9669913-1-1

Printed in Canada

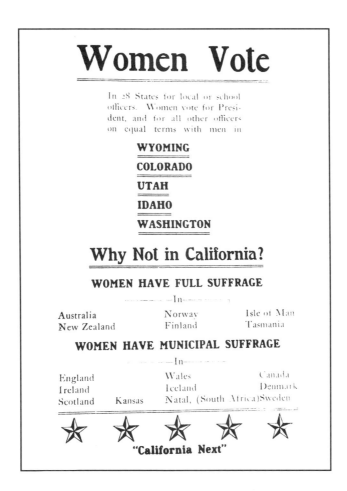

The Sixth Star: INTRODUCTION

While many books about California politics exist, surprisingly few trace the politics of California women. In the nineteenth century, San Francisco was the seat of the California women's movement, which began in 1868. From that vigorous movement came two benchmark elections, in 1896 and 1911, when California men voted on a woman's suffrage amendment to the state constitution. Aside from Selina Solomons' first hand account, *How We Won the Vote in 1911*, there is not even one book about the two campaigns for woman's suffrage. Such an omission poorly serves an understanding and appreciation of the women's movement in San

Francisco and the subsequent political history of California women.

In addition to mounting two campaigns to win their right to vote, women also challenged certain cultural myths about them and their circumstances. Taken in those days not as myths, but as truths, these myths became arguments to further curtail women's rights in other areas. Myths became legal arguments to exclude women from entrance to an institution of learning or from engaging in certain professions. Other myths explain why women should not have the right to vote. These were the leading myths:

1. A woman is morally superior to man: she, alone, embodies purity and goodness.
2. To engage in politics would taint and soil a woman's purity and goodness and furthermore would unsex her.
3. Women are inferior to men in terms of physical and mental development.
4. Women are more emotional than men.
5. For a woman to run a household, bear and rear children requires little or no education.
6. Every married woman would receive protection and support from her husband.

The next and last myth has taken much time to disprove, but during the nineteenth and twentieth centuries it was accepted as truth:

7. If women got the right to vote, they would shut down the liquor industry.

This last myth was a formidable obstacle facing the suffragists of this city. San Francisco had more liquor stores in it than any other city west of the Mississippi.

The liquor lobby had a tremendous hold in San Francisco in both cen-

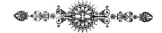

turies. Historically, this coastal city advanced its commercial trade industry through hospitality that included spirits, food and gracious people. As in the early times of the founding of the United States, taverns housed meetings of important people who forged political documents and crafted events crucial to our country's founding. This custom continued in San Francisco as it burst from a sleepy village into a boomtown flooded with gold seekers from all over the world. In San Francisco the saloon replaced the old tavern as a place to meet, make deals, develop contacts, and conduct business. San Francisco was a party town from its earliest days, and has retained that persona to the present day. Beyond this social custom involving good food and spirits was the fact that the city's economy and tax base became heavily reliant on its flourishing liquor business.

The other obstacle placed by San Francisco was the fact that it had a greater population than any city in the west and in the state. Considering the city's powerful liquor interests; its population dominance in the state; and the myth that voting women would shut down the liquor lobby, it was no wonder that the 1896 suffrage amendment failed.

To their credit, suffragists did not inflame the liquor issue by confronting it publicly. What they did underestimate was the population dominance San Francisco exerted over California in 1896. As San Francisco voted, so voted California.

In the twentieth century, as the population of the state increased and spanned out from San Francisco, San Francisco lost its population lead. When the city voted in 1911 against the suffrage amendment, the *Examiner* and the *Chronicle* automatically declared the suffrage amendment dead again. Even the city's suffragists forgot to dismiss the city's anticipated negative votes and to question its population lead. They thought suffrage had lost again. *The Call* reminded everyone that all California votes were not yet in. When the rest of California's votes affirmed the suffrage amendment, it was clear that San Francisco no longer spoke or voted for the entire state of California.

Additional forces and conditions contributed to the success of suffrage in 1911. The affluence gained from an economy fueled by the gold rush and silver strikes provided the families of the suffragists with money and resources for the cause. Women such as Miranda Lux, Jane Stanford, Phoebe Hearst, Mary Sperry, Mary McHenry Keith, Selina Solomons, Jane Knox Goodrich, Sarah Wallis, Laura de Force Gordon, Georgiana Bruce Kirby, Caroline Severance, Clara Shortridge Foltz, Emily Pitts Stevens and Ellen Clark Sargent underwrote California women's suffrage from one century to the next. The continuity of the leadership of these women was indispensable.

The labor union movement, particularly strong and unique in San Francisco, supported women's right to vote. At the Labor Day parade in San Francisco, in September, 1911, Samuel Gompers, head of the American Federation of Labor, publicly endorsed women's suffrage. The only majority vote for woman suffrage in 1911 was from the working class precincts.

At the dawn of the twentieth century, the progressive social-political reform movement in California, personified by such organizations as the anti-saloon associations, the Lincoln-Roosevelt Leagues, and the Nationalist (socialist) Clubs, permeated the state's politics. Almost the entire platform of the Lincoln-Roosevelt League became the proposed amendments to the state constitution voted on in the special election of October 10, 1911. The women's suffrage and women's eight-hour workday amendments passed with most of the other amendments.

When the automobile and the telephone emerged as devices nearly everyone could use, California women used these communication and mobility capabilities, especially in the 1911 suffrage campaign.

Particularly, members of the College Equal Suffrage League used their "Blue Liner" open roadster to motor through the countryside and farm towns. When the "Blue Liner" wheeled into town, parked at a corner and a college suffragist stood in the car and began to speak, soon a crowd of men gathered around. The target audience suffragists wanted to reach was men. The car attracted the right audience. This was good public relations. When votes were counted in 1911, college women thanked the California farmer who brought in the majority vote for women.

The telephone compressed this large state into a more manageable campaign system. With quick and efficient communication, the phone saved hours of travel and provided the 1911 suffragists with expanded means to conduct a statewide campaign.

These two political campaigns of 1896 and 1911 were not the only ways women fought for their rights and challenged the myths about them. In California women also founded clubs to discuss these issues and mounted the city's lecterns to disprove the myths. They initiated lawsuits challenging professions and institutions that denied them access. They crafted bills to replace discriminating laws and guided their passage into law. It took determination, energy, patience and time to disprove many of these myths and to gain their rights.

Each time a woman challenged a myth, she was political. Following the example of their ancestors who exercised their political acumen even before the Revolutionary War, California women joined the noble endeavor called politics and captured the Sixth Star for the suffragist banner.

Mae Kramer Silver

January 24, 2000

The Beginning Years: 1868-1895

THE INSPIRATION OF THE SUFFRAGE CAUSE

Laura deForce Gordon (1838-1907)

In the nineteenth century, Americans lauded their first lady of the podium, Anna Dickinson, a Quaker. But Laura deForce Gordon was California's own lady of the lectern. Credited with launching the suffrage movement with her speech in 1868, she was so fine a speaker, the Democrats hired her to stump for them. The Independent Party of San Joaquin County nominated her for the state senate and she ran in 1871. She became California's second woman lawyer in 1879. Tragically, she died before her beginning efforts for suffrage materialized.

Georgiana Bruce Kirby (1818-1887)

Invited in 1850 to Santa Cruz by her friend Eliza Farnham, Georgiana Bruce came, married, prospered and became an outspoken advocate for women's rights. She and Eliza scandalized the locals when they donned Turkish pants and rode horseback through the countryside. In 1871, when Emily Pitts Stevens chaperoned Susan B. Anthony and Elizabeth Cady Stanton to Santa Cruz, they were well met by Georgiana Kirby who arranged their speaking engagements and made sure their speeches were also well received, because Georgiana also reported for the *Santa Cruz Sentinel*. The radical, pro-suffrage presence in Santa Cruz prevailed through the 1896 election when Santa Cruz men voted a majority to amend the state constitution to give women the right to vote.

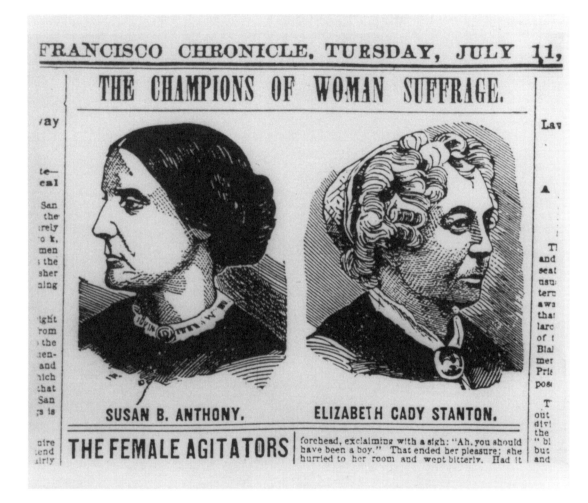

These unflattering pictures of Susan B. Anthony and Elizabeth Cady Stanton (similar to criminal wanted posters) on their one and only trip together to San Francisco in 1871, showed the *Chronicle*'s early anti-suffrage position. While labeled champions of suffrage, they were also called female agitators. Hurt and disappointed at the poor response from her first speech in the city, Susan B. Anthony cancelled the rest of her city speeches. Elizabeth Cady Stanton, however, had the city eating out of her hand. In those early times, even a charismatic orator like Mrs. Stanton could not convince the *Chronicle* that suffrage was a matter that all citizens, even women, aspired to and needed.

San Francisco Chronicle

SUNDAY.............. JULY 16, 1871.

☞ **The CHRONICLE has the Largest Circulation of any paper on the Pacific Coast.**

SIX-PAGE EDITION

Shall Women Vote?

ELIZABETH CADY STANTON and SUSAN B. ANTHONY have both expatiated on the rights of woman to suffrage, without acquainting the public with any cessentially new facts bearing upon the subject or bringing out any argument that has not been worn threadbare in the lecture-rooms of the Eastern States. Mrs. STANTON is an earnest advocate of this modern idea of female suffrage, and might make converts among those who listen to one side and believe all they hear and as resolutely refuse to listen to any refutation. We have heard nothing in the points made by either of these ladies to lead us to the conclusion that either man or woman would be benefited by the extension of the privilege of voting to the latter.

Woman Suffrage

(From the *San Francisco Chronicle*, Feb. 4, 1870)

Fiddle faddle! What's the use?
  You can't make her a man;
The great Creator fashioned her
  On quite another plan.
Man's joints are strong and firmly knit,
  His thews and sinews tough;
But woman is of daintier mould,
  And formed of finer stuff.

Men are the prose—the timber half
  Of this sad world of ours,
And women are the poetry
The sweet fern and the flowers.
Throughout the blessed Book this thought
Runs beautifully and clear,
That woman lives to sanctify,
To grace and to endear.

Don't let her, then; be smirched and soiled
  By mingling in the fray,
But keep her free from grosser acts
  To win her own sweet way.
Let purity remain her shield,
  Without a blot or stain,
To guard her mental bloom from taint
  Or touch of hand profane.

Forbid it, Heaven. Forbid it, Fate!
  Forbid it, men of sense,
That she herself should aid the plot
  To shame her own defense.
She is all glorious as she is—
  Why should the fretting few
Conspire to banish from her soul
  The fragrance and the dew?

Why take away her chiefest charm—
  The crown that's hers by right,
The quiet influence that compels
  Proud man to her own right?
She knows her power—why can't the sex
  Remain contented, then,
To rule us in the good old way?
Lord love us all—Amen!

Emily Pitts Stevens (1841-1906)

A woman with an incredibly high level of energy, Emily Pitts Stevens literally gathered the beginning threads of the women's movement and wove them into the cause for suffrage. She published the first journal for women's suffrage in the West. She was a member of the small group of July, 1869 patriots who formed the nucleus from which the California Woman Suffrage Association emerged in January, 1870. She and Laura deForce Gordon organized and hosted Susan B. Anthony's and Elizabeth Cady Stanton's one and only trip to San Francisco together in 1871. With a keen passion for the abuses women endured in an uncaring society, she formed organizations and provided printing opportunities to employ and train young women. As a teacher, she pioneered a public evening school for girls in 1867. An activist, a publisher, a businesswoman, a teacher, administrator, speaker and founder of organizations to benefit women and further suffrage, Emily Pitts Stevens' name should never be forgotten.

VOLUME VI—NUMBER 38
OFFICE—NO. 620 MONTGOMERY ST

SAN FRANCISCO, SUNDAY MORNING, APRIL 16, 1865.

TERMS—FOUR DOLLARS A YEAR
BY CARRIER, 10 CTS. PER MONTH

This is the masthead of the *California Sunday Mercury* that Emily Pitts Stevens bought and turned into the first written voice of suffrage in the West. Reflecting her highly charged energetic style, Mrs. Pitts Stevens renamed the journal three times before finally settling on *The Pioneer*. Within 1865 to 1870, Mrs. Pitts Stevens hired women to set type for her journal, promoted the all-woman Women's Co-operative Printing Union, and founded the Woman's Publishing Company.

Mrs. Julia Stevens Fish Schlesinger, editor and publisher of *The Carrier Dove*, formerly a Spiritualist weekly for children, expanded her Oakland publishing business to San Francisco in 1870. The Women's Co-operative Printing Union landed this plum of a commission. Soon, *The Carrier Dove* was second only to Emily Pitts Stevens' *The Pioneer*, the first suffrage publication in the West. *The Dove*, therefore, pushed forward women's right to vote in California.

THE CARRIER DOVE. A WEEKLY ILLUSTRATED JOURNAL.

THE SEVENTH YEAR OF PUBLICATION.

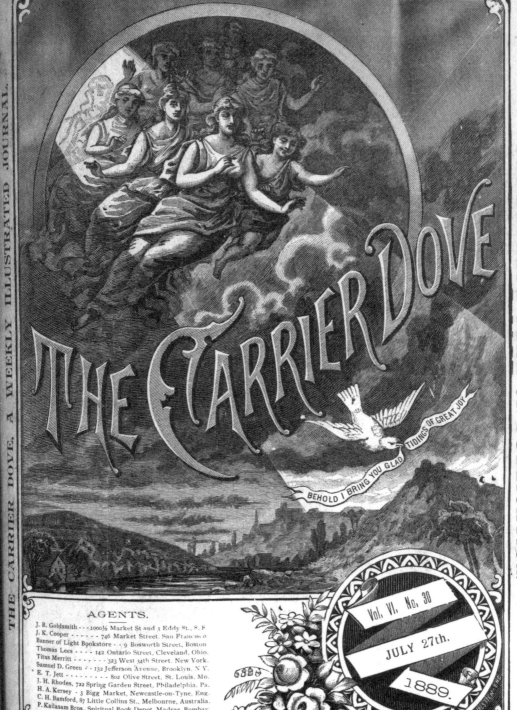

THE CARRIER DOVE

BEHOLD I BRING YOU GLAD TIDINGS OF GREAT JOY

Vol. VI, No. 30

JULY 27th,

1889.

AGENTS.

J. R. Goldsmith - - - 1000½ Market St and 3 Eddy St., S. F
J. K. Cooper - - - - - - 746 Market Street, San Francisco
Banner of Light Bookstore - - 9 Bosworth Street, Boston
Thomas Lees - - - - 142 Ontario Street, Cleveland, Ohio.
Titus Merritt - - - - - - 323 West 34th Street, New York.
Samuel D. Green - - 132 Jefferson Avenue, Brooklyn, N. Y.
E. T. Jett - - - - - - - - 802 Olive Street, St. Louis. Mo.
J. H. Rhodes, 722 Spring Garden Street, Philadelphia. Pa.
H. A. Kersey - 3 Bigg Market, Newcastle-on-Tyne, Eng.
C. H. Bamford, 87 Little Collins St., Melbourne, Australia.
P. Kallasam Bros., Spiritual Book Depot, Madras, Bombay.

Single Numbers, 10 cts.   Annual Subscription, $2.50.

OFFICE 841 MARKET STREET, SAN FRANCISCO, CAL.

In *Astrea*, Mrs Thorndyke wrote "Ode" to commemorate the first anniversary of the Woman's Suffrage Society, San Francisco, October, 1870. In May, 1869, the founders of the new National Woman Suffrage Association, Susan B. Anthony and Elizabeth Cady Stanton, appointed San Francisco's Elizabeth Schenck vice-president of the yet non-existent State Suffrage Association in California. The direction to Mrs. Schenck was clear: go found the state association! That summer when Mrs. Schenck and her radical friends heard Anna Dickinson lecture in San Francisco, they were aroused and inspired. The result was an "impromptu" founding, July 17, 1869, of the nucleus of the state suffrage association. President, Elizabeth Schenck; Vice-President, Emily Pitts Stevens; Recording Secretary, Nellie Hutchinson; Corresponding Secretary, Celia Curtis; Treasurer, Mrs. Corbett. After a series of fundraising lectures in the fall, the founding group organized a series of meetings, January 26-30, 1870, when the California Woman Suffrage Association formalized. President, Sarah M. Wallis; Vice-Presidents, J. A. Collins, Rev. C.G. Ames, Mary W. Coggins; Secretaries, Mrs. McGee, Mrs. Rider, Miss Perry; Treasurer, Mrs. Collins.

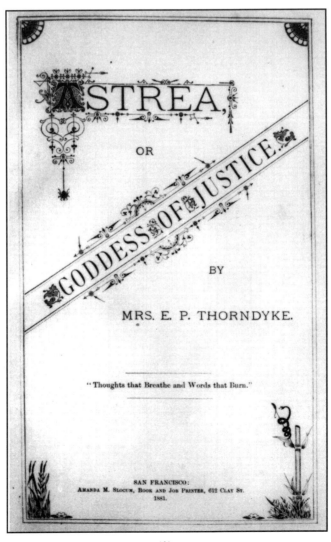

ODE

Written for the first anniversary of the Woman's Suffrage Society, San Francisco, October, 1870

ONE year ago to-day a Spartan band—
The truest, bravest, noblest of the land—
Assembled in this city by the sea,
Proclaiming boldly, *woman must be free!*
"The ballot gained, can aught else be denied!
Let bigots sneer, for *less* have martyrs died.
We see the future; here we count the cost;
The battle for the right is never lost."
From small beginnings see the forest grow,
The cities' tumult fill the vale below.
Old Ocean's heaving bosom covered o'er
With stately ships, while on the teeming shore
The din of labor, every freeman's pride,
Is moving commerce with a giant stride.

But 'tis a bolder theme we sing to-night;
These are but shadows to the morning light.
Lo woman comes! the ballot in her hand,
Opening the portal to a structure grand,
Enchantress of the future! free to steer
The Ship of State beyond the breakers clear;
Bringing her mother-love, sacred and pure.
To bear upon the laws, for error's cure;
Redeeming man from stern Mosaic rule
That stamps its impress on our modern school;
No more the subject ruled for selfish power,
The worshiped, fondled plaything of the hour,
But nature's queen in royal robes arrayed,
Her sceptre love, her throne the world's arcade.

So we, to-night, recount with glowing pen
The past years work, to be completd when
The Suffrage Ship is safely moored away
With victory sure, within some land-locked bay.
Good friends be cheered! the present is aglow
With hope and promise; all the past doth show
A prophecy that time will render sure,
Then watch and work and patiently endure.
Humanity with bleeding heart doth plead
For *woman's* influence in this hour of need;
The fabled story of poor Adam's fall
Has reached a climax, in this modern thrall;
The subject, woman, and the master, man,
Hath brought the Nations under fearful ban.

We ask a hearing; here we press our claim
To our own birthright in a woman's name,
Give us the Ballot; with it comes the power
To right old wrongs; then consecrate this hour
To woman's effort; all her latent strength
Like pent-up forces, must assert itself,
The noble river in its majesty
Among green glades while sweeping to the sea,
Dammed and diverted from its native course
By artificial barriers of force,
O'erflows its banks and inundates the land,
Demoralizing all the work of man.
So woman's nature, damned by man-made laws,
O'ersteps all bounds, and man her brother, draws
Into the vortex where they both must fall,
Cursed by the tyranny that crushes all.
Let nobler motives move the people now,
Before whose mandates even kinds must bow,
Till every woman in Earth's broad domain
Shall rend her fetters and cast off her chain.

LABOR IS WORSHIP

WORK, earnest woman, work!
 Nor lay your armor by;
The morning brings a golden light,
 Born of the evening sky.

Work, earnest souls, nor faint
 Before your task is done,
The victor may the spoils enjoy,
 Your work is scarce begun.

Take up the tuneful song,
 Heard by the favored few
Whose souls to music are attuned,
 The brave alone are true.

Say not the way is dark,
 The end is yet afar;
Work in the present, trusting still
 To truth's bright guiding star.

There's fainting souls to cheer,
 Oppression's hand to stay,
The dust of error gathers still
 About the pilgrim's way.

Then let your minds illume
 The misty troubled dream,
Where ignorance, with blinding force,
 Pollutes life's flowing stream.

The BALLOT! who may know
 How a woman's hand will bless,
When vested with a freeman's right
 Her mandate to express.

Then keep the goal in view,
 Inspiring heart and hand,
Let woman's birthright be secured
 O'er all this favored land.

The mountains and the vales
 Are speaking to the sea,
In language potent as the storm,
 "Our daughters shall be free."

Free as the mind is free,
 Speaking to high and low,
A voice reverberates the land,
 "Let thou my people go."

The Spiritualist book, *Astrea*, written by Mrs. Thorndyke (1885) contained this poem, clearly showing the tie between Spiritualism and suffrage. The religious overtones of "Labor is Worship," the plaintive plea for freedom and liberty, and the agony of bondage all reveal the passion for suffrage in nineteenth century San Francisco.

EVERY DESCRIPTION OF

PRINTING

NEATLY EXECUTED, AT THE

Women's Co-operative Printing Union,

424 MONTGOMERY STREET,

SAN FRANCISCO, CAL.

In this advertisement for the Women's Co-operative Printing Union in Carrie Young's *West Coast Journal*, May 18, 1870, note the name, L. Curtis, right at the hemline of the printer's skirt. As teenagers, Leila Curtis and her sister Mary became fascinated with the process of copper engraving. Both parents, having a background in engraving, encouraged their daughters' interest. Soon the sisters opened an engraving shop in the carriage house of their San Francisco home at 1117 Pine Street. Mary became the draughtsman, i.e., the artist, and Leila, the block-cutter. That endeavor led to a shop downtown and eventually a partnership called Crane and Curtis (1871). Mary withdrew from the business when she married Thomas Richardson in 1869. Her life's work became painting; the Richardson house became a mecca for artists and writers. Mary Curtis Richardson became a well known, and very successful portraitist. When Leila married the New York portraitist Benoni Irving (1886), it was clear both sisters again, as in their early life, shared the rich, productive world of art. Another fascinating part of the Curtis history pertains, possibly, to mother Ceilia. A Celia Curtis, note the different name spelling, was one of the July, 1869 patriots who pioneered the California Woman's Suffrage Association. Could it be that Ceilia and Celia were one and the same early suffragist in San Francisco?

Ellen Clark Sargent

(1826-1911)

Ellen Clark Sargent (1826-1911)

With her husband, Senator Aaron A. Sargent (Nevada City, Cal.), Ellen Clark Sargent became an early major link between suffragists in California and Washington, D.C. The Sargents established an early relationship with Susan B. Anthony. Senator Sargent was the first person in the entire Congress who uttered the word "suffrage" and wrote a suffrage amendment to the U.S. Constitution. In 1872, when Ellen Sargent became secretary to the National Suffrage Association, her husband went "to bat" for Susan B. Anthony who was jailed for registering to vote—a federal offense. Actually, she was fined for registering to vote, and when she refused to pay the fine, she was incarcerated. Senator Sargent went to President Grant to intercede on behalf of Miss Anthony and, in effect, "sprung" the great lady from jail.

The Sargent's home, wherever it was, was always open to all suffragists. At the time of the 1896 campaign, when Mrs. Sargent was president of the California Woman Suffrage Association, the Sargent home on Folsom Street was one of the main head-quarters for the suffrage vote. In 1888, when Julia Ward Howe came west to visit her sister in Marin County, she met at the home of Ellen Sargent, along with Phoebe A. Hearst, Sarah Dix Hamlin, Emma Sutro Merritt, M.D. and others. This was the group that founded the city's first woman's club, the Century Club, which still flourishes at 1355 Franklin St.

The impact of the Sargent family, including children George and Elizabeth, on the suffrage movement in California was inestimable. Only a few weeks, indeed, days, before women won their right to vote on October 10, 1911, Ellen Clark Sargent died. An unusual memorial, the first given to a woman at that time, was held, with Governor Hiram Johnson honoring her achievements in Union Square, San Francisco.

Marietta Beers-Stow (1835–1902)

This was Marietta Beers-Stow's pensive picture as it appeared in her 1876 book, *Probate Confiscation*, her personal exposé of the horrors and inequities of the California Probate Court system, which she dubbed "the high court of prostitution." Having just lost her husband, she was thrown into legal limbo, as the Probate Court, creditors, etc., had first draw on her inheritance from her husband. All her furniture, even her writing desk, was confiscated for appraisal and she was reduced to asking a judge for money to cover her medical expenses. She approached the state legislature with a new law governing widows and children. She exclaimed,

"The Probate Court grows fat on the meat of the
starving widow and children.
I've had wrongs
To stir a fever in the blood of age,
Or make the infant's sinews strong as steel."

Still grieving for her husband at the time of this picture, Mrs. Stow wore a picture pin of her deceased husband, a customary practice of a widow active in mourning. In 1882, Marietta Beers-Stow became the first woman to run for governor in the state of California. In 1884, she ran as vice-president of the United States to Belva Lockwood (Washington, D.C.), running for president.

The 1895 California Woman's Congress Association
Board Members and staff

Left to right, standing: Mrs. Louise A. Sorbier, Mrs. W. E. Hall, Mrs. Charlotte Perkins Gilman, Mrs. George T. Gaden (Minne V.); seated, Mrs. Garrison Gerst, Mrs. Ada Van Pelt, Mrs. Sarah B. Cooper, Nellie Blessing Eyster. The famous feminist intellectual Charlotte Perkins Gilman was the staff person hired by Board President Sarah Cooper. In this picture Mrs. Gilman stood behind Mrs. Cooper, her benefactor, who sought out Mrs. Gilman to organize the first congresses. As a single mother with a young child and an ailing mother, Mrs. Gilman was also strapped for funds. Recognized for her talent and genius by local writers and suffragists, Charlotte Perkins Gilman received good support and encouragement from the San Francisco community. Mrs. Gilman's gaze in this picture—at Mrs. Cooper and not the photographer—perhaps showed her appreciation of Mrs. Cooper's help.

Mm. Sorbier's foresight and sense of history left us her papers, images, and scrapbooks covering suffrage from one century to the other as invaluable resources for research at the California Historical Society.

WAITING TO HEAR THE PLEAS IN FAVOR OF WOMAN'S RIGHT TO VOTE.
(Long before the opening of the doors of the hall a large number of enthusiastic followers of the Woman's Congress assembled on the steps and discussed among themselves the growth of the movement and the force of the arguments set forth by the leading speakers of the day before.)

"The Hand that Rocks the Cradle Rears the Patriot" was the subtheme of the 1896 Woman's Congress theme of "Woman and Government". The Pacific Coast Woman's Press Association created the West Coast Woman's Congress Association that sponsored four women's congresses from 1894 through 1897. Each year, in late April or early May, congresses convened in San Francisco; the speakers and their subjects determined a specific theme. Accomplished women from the West Coast spoke for days, from morning till night. The Congresses were a smash hit, with women jamming every inch of space to get in and hear. The 1896 theme aroused California women to go for the vote that November.

Sarah B. Cooper (1836–1896)

The untimely death of suffragist Sarah Brown Cooper on the eve of her 60th birthday stunned San Franciscans. Mrs. Cooper deftly organized events and institutions on behalf of children and women in the city. She founded the Golden Gate Kindergarten Association, a consortium of 50 kindergartens throughout the city. With outstanding administrative and leadership skills, she was vice-president of the Century Club, president and vice-president of the prestigious Women's Press Association, treasurer of the World Federation of Women's Clubs, director of the S.F. Associated Charities board, and president for two years of the West Coast Woman's Congress board. She had recently turned her attention to the suffrage cause. Undoubtedly, had she lived, she would have added her indelible talents and dedication to the movement.

As an example of the unseen work of sisterhood in early San Francisco, Miranda Lux, a woman of substantial means, aware of Mrs. Cooper's unique value to the community, became her patron. She supported her and her daughter Hattie with a comfortable home and provisions. In this way, Mrs. Cooper devoted her full time and energy on behalf of causes for San Francisco children and women. She continued that sisterly circle of support when she singled out Mrs. Charlotte Perkins Gilman and employed her to organize the first women's congress on the West Coast.

THE BIFURCATED SKIRT

THE BEST DIVIDED SKIRT.

In 1892 at the posh Palace Hotel in downtown San Francisco, Anna Janess Miller, editor and owner of her own magazine, *Janess Miller Monthly*, hosted a fashion show of her bifurcated skirts. Through her periodical, she sold patterns and designs of the divided skirt, all the rage with the women's bicycle set. Curiously, in 1851, another Miller, Elizabeth Smith Miller, cousin to Elizabeth Cady Stanton, originated the first woman's pants creation, the bloomer costume. The women's magazine *Lily* advocated the bloomer as a response to women's concern for the safety of wearing long skirts and the unsanitary conditions of long trailing skirts in contact with mud and dirt of unpaved streets. The bicycle craze that hit San Francisco around 1895 provoked a need for a safe tangle-free costume for the new woman who wanted her own wheels, another sign of a liberated, emancipated woman who wanted to move in her own time, rhythm and place.

The Fourth Star:
THE 1896 CAMPAIGN

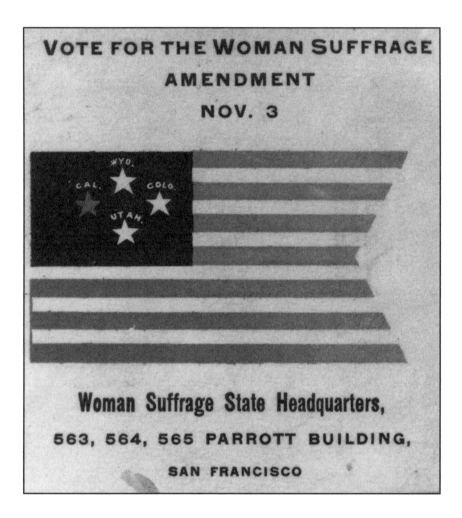

In 1896, California women hoped to capture their right to vote, thereby adding their Fourth Star to the woman's suffrage banner. Women could vote in Wyoming (1869), Colorado (1893) and Utah (1896).

"WOMAN'S PLACE IS IN THE HOME"

Members of the National Woman Suffrage Association came to San Francisco in 1896 to craft the 1896 campaign. Two California women, Ellen Clark Sargent and Mary McHenry Keith, headed families that unselfishly devoted resources and time to suffrage from the beginning to the end in California. Their constant leadership insured the continuity, strength and success of the suffrage movement in the state.

clockwise from lower left

1. Sarah B. Cooper
2. Mrs. E.O. Smith*
3. Ellen C. Sargent
4. Mary Garrett
5. Mrs. Goodrich*
6. Mary Swift*

7. Dr. Anna H. Shaw
8. Winifred Harper
9. Ida H. Harper
10. Susan B. Anthony
11. Mary McHenry Keith

educated guess by author

WILL LEAVE THEM NO CHANCE TO ESCAPE

Woman Suffragists Will Charge on the Democrats From Every Point of the Compass.

SACRAMENTO, June 16.—The condition of things here, so far as the cause of equal rights is concerned, has changed materially from what it was, say, four years ago. Then we had received but little encouragement in our efforts to interest delegates in favor of declaring for the pending amendments to the State Constitution. Now we have assurances from scores of men who are entitled to seats in the Convention hall that they will support any platform plank or resolution favoring the cause we are to do battle for.

The leaflet, or pamphlet, sent out by "The Examiner" this morning is the best thing of the kind that I have ever seen, and the good it has done us cannot be measured by words. It contained testimonials from Colorado that are entirely new and of great value to our cause at this particular time. We, who are the workers in the cause, know how to appreciate these things, because we know the effect they have for good or evil.

Just where we will stand before this Convention cannot be determined until the Committee on Platform and Resolutions has been organized and we have had the opportunity to present to it our claims for recognition. In the meantime it is not too much to say that we have secured the pledges of many individual delegates, and that some entire delegations have pledged themselves to support a woman suffrage plank in the party platform. I may also say that we have some friends on the committee, and we are all but certain of some sort of recognition.

Our wish is, of course, to have the committee adopt the plank we have prepared and will present for its consideration. Failing in this, we expect our friends to prepare a minority report, which will be presented to the convention. By this means we will get the subject before that body, and it will then depend upon the votes of the whole body of delegates to either accept or reject.

During the months of July and August we shall send speakers into every town and hamlet in the State of California. Aside from this, we expect invitations to speak in all party meetings on the woman-suffrage plank. Our women orators will be known by their advocacy of the proposed amendment and for nothing else. They will be instructed to refer in no way to any party measure or party grievance. In fact, so far as our campaign is concerned, we shall keep ourselves entirely outside any and all issues of the various political parties, and confine our attention wholly and solely to the cause of equal rights.

If the Democratic party fails to indorse the plank that we propose to present to this convention, it will, by so doing, lose the friendship of a great majority of the women of this State. As the case now stands, the other three political parties have, by adopting our plank, opened the doors of their meetings to our speakers. Should the Democrats fail to do likewise, it stands to reason that they will thereby alienate the sympathy of the Democratic women of the State. One-seventh of the taxes in California are paid by women, and it is only natural that they should wish to have some voice in the matter of the expenditure of money. Three political parties have declared themselves as being in favor of granting them this right. It now remains to be seen whether or not the Democratic party will do as much.   SUSAN B. ANTHONY.

In the summer of 1896, the leaders of the national suffrage movement came to California to show California suffragists how to conduct their first campaign to convince men to vote for a state constitutional amendment for women's suffrage. Susan B. Anthony led the way, and the California suffrage leaders followed and learned how to present their case for suffrage to the men's political parties. "Charging the Democrats from every point of the compass" was a marvelous metaphor, but it did not budge the Democrats, who never included suffrage in their platform. Although the article by Susan B. Anthony was shortened (by this writer) to fit the page structure, the writing is vintage Anthony, showing her style and approach to politics.

This familiar photograph of suffragists still remains, since 1896, fully uncaptioned. First row, left to right: Lucy Anthony, Dr. Anna Shaw, Susan B. Anthony, Ellen C. Sargent, Mary Hays; second row, left to right: Ida Husted Harper, Selina Solomons, Carrie Chapman Catt, Anne Bidwell. This picture shows the national figures—note the tiny flags pinned on their dresses–and the locals, i.e., the 1896 campaign team.

Mary McHenry Keith (1855-1947)

As the first woman graduate of the Hastings School of the Law (San Francisco) in 1881, Mary McHenry Keith used her knowledge of the law for a commitment to women's suffrage that spanned two centuries. William Keith, an ardent suffragist and brilliant landscape artist, and Mrs. Keith opened their home to members of the national and local suffrage movement from beginning to end. The Keiths were personal friends of Susan B. Anthony. It was to Mrs. Keith that Miss Anthony entrusted the leadership for the 1911 suffrage campaign in the state. In 1911, two women who had a relationship to law and the Hastings School of the Law, were two key suffrage leaders in the state. Mary McHenry Keith was the Northern California leader; Clara Shortridge Foltz led Southern California.

Her hometown, Berkeley, called her "Berkeley's Mother of Suffrage." As the only town in the counties of Alameda and San Francisco that voted for suffrage—not only in 1896 but again in 1911—one might say that Mary McHenry Keith had mothered Berkeley well. In this picture, Mrs. Keith wore a yellow silk rose boutonniere, a symbol of the suffrage movement.

Mary McHenry Keith

possibly at the time of her graduation from the Hastings School of the Law.

RECEPTION . . . . .

THE

. . . Woman Suffrage Association

Requests the pleasure of your company at the

HOTEL NADEAU

On Saturday Evening, April 27th, 1895,

FROM EIGHT TO ELEVEN.

PRESIDENT FOR THE EVENING:
Hon. J. E. McComas, Pomona.

RECEPTION COMMITTEE:
Mesdames Mary E. Threldkeld, Sarah A. McClees, M. Burton Williamson,
Hester A. Harland, Margaret V. Longley.
Misses Harland, Teal, Hazletine, North and James.

(over)

The men of Berkeley, California grabbed hold of the woman suffrage cause and never let go. In the 1896 election, Berkeley was the only place in San Francisco and Alameda counties that gave a majority vote for the suffrage amendment. When the franchise vote was put to Berkeley men again in 1911, they once again voted in favor of the women's suffrage amendment.

Political Equality!

AN ADDRESS AT

WRIGHTS HALL

—BY—

MRS. HESTER A. HARLAND,

State Organizer Woman's Suffrage Associations,

Monday Evening, Nov. 18th,
AT 7-80 O'CLOCK

EVERYBODY INVITED

Berkeley resident Hester A. Harland (1857-1940) was an effective, effervescent speaker and organizer from one century into the next. As testimony of her sense of history, she left a fine collection of clippings, campaign ephemera, letters and notes one can read at the Bancroft Library. This handbill for the 1896 campaign reflects her high spirit and energy.

Clara Shortridge Foltz (1849-1934)

   A southern California suffrage leader and California's first woman lawyer, Clara
Shortridge Foltz figured prominently in the 1911 campaign. After her family moved
to the Santa Clara area, she began to read for the law. She wrote the Woman Lawyers'
Bill, and with her friend Laura deForce Gordon, she championed the bill which gave
women the right to practice law in California. She sued Hastings School of the Law
for not admitting women and with Laura deForce Gordon, convincingly argued the
case in court. They won. When she moved to Los Angeles, Clara Foltz devoted the full
resources of her law practice to suffrage. Since it was the votes from the men of Los
Angeles and the "cow counties" that created the majority vote for suffrage, the influence of California's "Portia of the Pacific" can never be underestimated.

NO SALOONS OPEN, BUT——

THE ARGUMENT GREW HEATED.

THIRST CAN FIND A WAY.

The *Examiner* characterized the November, 1896 election as orderly and quiet. Inter-spersed in this same article were Jimmy Swinnerton's cartoons that showed perhaps a different behavior linked to liquor consumption. His cartoons were worth a thousand words.

This campaign badge was silky yellow, fringed at both ends. Yellow, or more precisely, California gold, was the official color of the suffrage movement and campaigns in California. On November 3, 1896, a majority of 20,000 San Francisco men voted against the proposed amendment to the state constitution giving California women the right to vote. The amendment listed last, No. 6 on the ballot, attracted, according to the San Francisco *Examiner*, "...many more votes...than any of the other 5 amendments proposed." Implied in this observation was the idea that the heavy hand of the liquor establishment had directed even the most inebriated fingers to mark an "X" on the last box of the amendment ballot. Suffragists had tried to prevent their amendment from being either first or last and secured, they thought, an agreement from the appropriate state official to keep their amendment in the middle of the list. They were dismayed and shocked to see their amendment listed last.

Smarting from this defeat, California suffragists met two days later, November 5 and 6, at Golden Gate Hall, San Francisco. Their eyes were on the next campaign. The fight was not over.

Oct, 1907 *Portrait Mrs. Koeth*

SUFFRAGE CONVENTION NUMBER

Vol. I. Official Journal of the Washington and California Equal Suffrage Associations. No. 14

WESTERN WOMAN

Edited by Laura Bride Powers

Equal Suffrage News
Civics-Local Politics
Clubs and Club Women
Art and the Artists

Worthwhile Books
Foyer and Footlights
Good Roads-Motoring
Happenings

SAN FRANCISCO, OCTOBER, 1907

TEN CENTS THE COPY

Monthly Advocate Of Political Equality And Allied Interests

THE ABBEY

MILL VALLEY,
CALIFORNIA

IDEALLY SITUATED ON WOODED SIDE OF MT. TAMALPAIS

MOST ALLURING SPOT IN MARIN COUNTY

ABBIE C. HOWE, PROPRIETOR

Program

Friday, October 24th

9 a. m. to 9:30 a. m.

EXECUTIVE COMMITTEE MEETING

10:00 a. m.

DELEGATE MEETING

Prayer.. Mrs. GEO. HAIGHT

READING OF MINUTES

ANNOUNCEMENT OF COMMITTEES

REPORTS OF OFFICERS

REPORTS OF COUNTY SOCIETIES

Friday Afternoon, October 24th

2 p. m.

SUSAN B. ANTHONY...Greetings
Dr. DOROTHEA MOORE.......................................Municipal Office
Dr. MINORA KIBBE....................From Partial to Impartial Suffrage
Miss ELIZABETH MURRAY...........Recitation, Sally Ann's Experience
          By Anna Calvert Hall
MR. T. G. SAWKINS..How Universal Suffrage was secured in Australia
Mrs. J. M. REYNOLDS..............Greetings—Woman's Socialist Union
Mrs. FLORENCE KENDALL.............................Consumers' League
Mrs. LUCRETIA N. TAYLOR..Some Latter Day Aspects of the Suffrage
                  Movement
Mrs. J. G. LEMMON ....Forestry
MRS. FLORENCE JACKSON STODDARD..................Adult Education

Friday Evening, October 24th

8 p. m.

HARMONY QUINTETTE .... "*Estudiantina*"

Mrs. A. T. FLETCHER   Mrs. JOHN MADDEN
Miss GUSSIE NEWPORT   Mrs. ROBERT LLOYD
Miss EDITH ADAMS, at the Piano

BENJAMIN FAY MILLS .... Address—What if Women Should Vote
HARMONY QUINTETTE .... "*Annie Laurie*"

Saturday, October 25th

10 a. m.

REPORT OF CREDENTIALS COMMITTEE

REPORT OF CHAIRMAN ON ORGANIZATION

AMENDMENTS TO THE CONSTITUTION

ELECTION OF OFFICERS

REPORT OF RESOLUTIONS COMMITTEE

Saturday, October 25th

2 p. m.

Dr. DAVID STARR JORDAN ...What the 20th Century Demands of our Young Women
Mrs. A. T. FLETCHER .... Vocal Solo
Mrs. WILLIAM KEITH .... Co-Education
Miss ADA L. A. MURCOTT ....Status of Women in Australia
Miss MABEL CLARE CRAFT....Trend of Women's Clubs toward Public Service
Miss SUSANNE R. PATCH.................... Library Work in California
Mrs. M. E. IONIS..Community Property Rights of Husband and Wife

Susan B. Anthony was back in San Francisco in 1902 as the lead speaker, giving greetings to the delegates of the annual convention of the California Woman Suffrage Association at Century Hall, 1215 Sutter, between Polk and Van Ness. Note the messages at the top of each page of the program: "In victory only do the brave cease to fight," and, "Governments derive their just powers from the consent of the governed."

This was California's suffrage leader Mary McHenry Keith's badge to the national convention of the National American Woman Suffrage Association in Portland, Oregon. NAWSA celebrated Sacajawea's remarkable and heroic contributions to the success of the Lewis and Clark Expedition. Not only a linguist and a scout, but with a clear mind and quick hand, it was Sacajawea who retrieved Lewis and Clark's journals during an accident when their canoe capsized.

NELLIE HOLBROOK BLINN.

Nellie Holbrook Blinn

A crackerjack of a speaker, this blonde, blue-eyed suffragist defied the oft-used stereotype of the suffragist as a dour old woman. A teacher at the age of 13, she matured into a powerful speaker who could project her voice to the last row of an out-door gathering. Her stage presence could counter gracefully even the fiercest badger-ing from anti-suffragists in the audience. She was so winning and capable, politicians hired her to campaign for them.

Her talents included organizing. In San Francisco, at the 1906 suffrage convention, overflowing with enthusiastic women undaunted by the presence of the devastation of the great earthquake and fire, Mrs. Blinn proposed reorganizing the entire state in the chain-of-command structure that served the Los Angeles area so successfully during the 1896 election.

Leading a march August 27, 1908, in Oakland of three hundred of the most influential California suffragists were: (left to right) Lillian Harris Coffin, Mrs. Theodore Pinther, Jr. and Mrs. Theodore Pinther, Sr. Mrs. Pinther, Jr. held the silk banner she sewed in California gold and Pacific blue. Although this impressive march, organized by Lillian Coffin, had little noticeable effect on the Republicans, it undoubtedly galvanized the suffragists for their next try for the vote.

Lillian Harris Coffin

As bold and brainy as she was beautiful, Lillian Harris Coffin was the chief lobby-ist for the California Equal Woman Suffrage Association, aka California Woman Suffrage Association. She knew the legislators well and they knew her. She rarely for-got promises for suffrage made by legislators, and then held them to their word...or else. She taught other members of the Suffrage Association how to lobby, to organ-ize, and to exert their leadership on behalf of suffrage. Suffragists never forgot her marvelous march in downtown Oakland to the state Republican convention.

How We Won the Vote in California

By

Selina Solomons

Selina Solomons (1862-1942)

This pose by Selina Solomons said a lot about her fiery, in-your-face sassiness, liveliness, and unconventional and bright spirit. She said, "October 10, 1911 proved to be the greatest day in my life...."

Selina Solomons was a pioneer in suffrage, serving the cause from one century to the next. Also, she ventured into suffrage leadership, an activity most Jewish women passed by in favor of club participation. She lectured on the subject "The Matriarchate" at the Woman's Congress, May 25, 1895. Again, she distinguished herself as a leader, in that she was one of a handful of women speakers who held no degree higher than a high school diploma. She had established her credibility as a feminist.

Selina began her version of the 1911 suffrage campaign a year earlier than the official one! On February 15, 1910, she opened the Votes-for-Women Club in a large

Justice to California Women

WOMEN VOTE on some questions in Massachusetts, New York, Ohio, Illinois Kentucky and in 26 other states.

WOMEN VOTE equally with men in Wyoming, Colorado, Utah, Idaho and Washington.

Why not in California?

loft in the retail district of San Francisco, at 315 Sutter Street. The space housed a rest room, reading room, serving room and kitchen. For five cents, one could lunch from a tempting buffet. Aimed specifically at the local women clerks and salesgirls, it also attracted women shoppers.

Once she had the place, Selina turned it into a headquarters for suffrage. With no endowment, she managed the Club as self-supporting. She organized a men's auxiliary, the membership to which required dues. A suffrage bazaar, during the holidays, sold merchandise. A women's congress presented scheduled lecturers, but there were impromptu speakers as well. Suffrage posters hung on the walls; suffrage reading material abounded; plays were performed. She produced handbills, postcards and handouts with the suffrage message. Selina was a dynamo. And she organized pro-suffrage demonstrations.

As part of the campaign the next year, Selina wrote her suffrage play, *The Girl from Colorado,* supposedly while she was resting in Yosemite Valley, likely at her brother Theodore's cabin. Five characters engaged in a light romantic comedy about Aunty Suffridge's conversion from non-suffrage to suffrage. The New Women Publishing Company in San Francisco printed the play. The play was staged repeatedly during the last days of the suffrage struggle.

On the fateful day of the election, October 10, 1911, Gail Laughlin, a Colorado attorney and chair of the Election Day Committee noted fraudulent voting in North Beach, often linked to the inebriation of either voters or voting officials. As predicted, San Francisco men voted suffrage down for the second time. But all the rest of the votes of the state were not yet in. San Francisco suffragists held their breath for good news.

Selina recalled, "We had kept back our womanish tears on that Black Wednesday. Now we gave free rein to our emotions, in both manly and womanly fashion, with handshaking and back-slapping, as well as hugging and kissing one another." The ordeal was exhausting and "...not until a month later could we summon the nervous energy to plan and carry out a celebration of our own on a fitting scale—a big jubilee banquet, the last and best of all suffrage banquets held in San Francisco."

Selina Solomons published *How We Won the Vote* in 1912.

Votes for Women   Votes for Women

Equal Suffrage Map of the United States, 1909

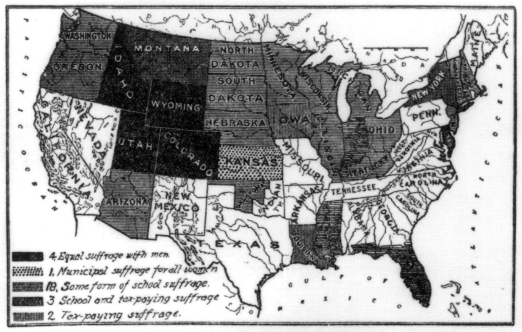

4. Equal suffrage with men.
1. Municipal suffrage for all women.
10. Some form of school suffrage.
3. School and tax-paying suffrage.
2. Tax-paying suffrage.

For the Long Work Day
For the Taxes We Pay
For the Laws We Obey
We Want Something to Say.

Men and women vote on equal terms for all officers, even for presidential electors,
in **4** of the United States. In **25** other states women have partial suffrage.

California Women have no Votes

Printed by California Equal Suffrage Ass'n   Price, one-half cent each
Address: Votes for Women, 611 Gilman St., Palo Alto

When the College Equal Suffrage League offered a prize of $50 for a Votes-for-Women poster, Bertha Boye won it with this grand entry.

Buy a Broom!

Charlotte Perkins Gilman took the popular 1860's song, "Buy a Broom," gave it words and named it "Another Star," referring to California as the sixth star in the suffrage banner. The original words to the song parody a Bavarian drinking song with hausfrau ideas about "brushing away insects that annoy you," and sweeping all "vexatious intruders away." Leave it to Mrs. Gilman's inventive, playful mind to take a song about sweeping, brushing and cleaning and nearly turn it into a marching song about the woman's ballot. The concept that women would clean up the world of politics with their vote, like cleaning one's own house of vexatious creatures with a broom, became a sub-theme of the women's suffrage movement. An idea we still hear today.

This is the original songsheet, ca. 1860, of "Buy A Broom," the Bavarian Girls' song, to which Charlotte Perkins Gilman wrote "Another Star." Referring to the sixth star in the suffragists' banner, this song became an official song of the 1911 California women's suffrage campaign.

Another Star

Tune: "**Buy a Broom**"

Charlotte Perkins Gilman in The ForeRunner for March, 1911

There are five a-light before us,
In the flag flying o'er us,
There'll be six on next election—
    We bring a new star!
We are coming like the others,
Free Sisters, Free Brothers,
In the pride of our affection
    For California.

Chorus
A ballot for the Lady!
For the Home and for the Baby!
Come, vote ye for the Lady,
    The Baby, the Home!

Star of hope and Star of Beauty!
Of Freedom! of Duty!
Star of Childhood's new protection,
    That rises so high!
We will work for it together,
In the golden, gay weather,
And we'll have it next election,
    Or we will know why.

Chorus
A ballot for the Lady!
For the Home and for the Baby!
Come, vote ye for the Lady,
    The Baby, the Home!

Adopted by the Executive Board of California Equal Suffrage Assn.
as an official campaign song.   Printed in Palo Alto.    3

Elizabeth Lowe Watson

As President of the California Equal Suffrage Association, aka the California Woman Suffrage Association, from 1909 to 1911, Mrs. Watson saw her dream come true for California women. Earlier, her personal quest for emancipation led her to become a pastor in the First Spiritualist Union of San Francisco (1896). For her friend and ardent suffragist, Georgiana Bruce Kirby, she delivered the funeral oration in Santa Cruz (1887).

Berkeley Suffrage Campaign Headquarters
2515 BANCROFT WAY

You are cordially invited to come to our Headquarters and identify yourself with the campaign through which we aim to secure full citizenship for the women of California.

As the Amendment to the State Constitution granting Suffrage to Women is to be voted upon at a special election on October tenth we have but a few months in which to work. Will you give us all possible help, and personally take part in the movement which aims to make California a broader, better and more REPRESENTATIVE STATE?

WE NEED YOU

Headquarters open daily.

Open meetings every Wednesday afternoon at 2:30.

Literature for circulation.

Very truly yours,

(MRS.) HESTER HARLAND.

ASSOCIATE COUNCIL.

Mrs. Geo. W. Haight
Mrs. Wm. Keith
Mrs. John Snook
Mrs. Fred G. Athearn
Mrs. Irving M. Scott, Jr.
Dr. Helen Waterman
Mrs. Samuel C. Haight
Mrs. Aaron C. Schloss
Mrs. T. B. Sears
Mrs. C. C. Hall
Mrs. Frank F. Bunker

VOTES FOR WOMEN!
THE WOMAN'S REASON.
BECAUSE

BECAUSE women must obey the laws just as men do,
> They should vote equally with men.

BECAUSE women pay taxes just as men do, thus supporting the government,
> They should vote equally with men.

BECAUSE women suffer from bad government just as men do,
> They should vote equally with men.

BECAUSE mothers want to make their children's surroundings better,
> They should vote equally with men.

BECAUSE over 5,000,000 women in the United States are wage workers and their health and that of our future citizens are often endangered by evil working conditions that can only be remedied by legislation,
> They should vote equally with men.

BECAUSE women of leisure who attempt to serve the public welfare should be able to support their advice by their votes,
> They should vote equally with men.

BECAUSE busy housemothers and professional women cannot give such public service, and can only serve the state by the same means used by the busy man—namely, by casting a ballot,
> They should vote equally with men.

BECAUSE women need to be trained to a higher sense of social and civic responsibility, and such sense developes by use,
> They should vote equally with men.

BECAUSE women are consumers, and consumers need fuller representation in politics,
> They should vote equally with men.

BECAUSE women are citizens of a government **of** the people, **by** the people and **for** the people, **and women are people.**
> They should vote equally with men.

EQUAL SUFFRAGE FOR MEN AND WOMEN.

WOMEN Need It.
MEN Need It.
The STATE Needs It.

WHY?

BECAUSE

Women Ought To GIVE Their Help.
Men Ought To HAVE Their Help.
The State Ought To USE Their Help.

WOMAN SUFFRAGE PARTY
OF THE CITY OF NEW YORK
Headquarters: Room 212 Metropolitan Life Building

WOMAN SHOULD VOTE
SHE IS MOTHER AND TEACHER
VOTE FOR AMENDMENT NO. 8

Phillips & Van Orden Co., 509-511 Howard st. S. F.

Minna O'Donnell

Minna O'Donnell represented the vigorous level of labor's support on behalf of woman suffrage in San Francisco from 1909-1911, when the Union Labor Party's candidate, Patrick McCarthy was mayor of the city. He came out for woman suffrage. Louise LaRue, head of Waitresses' Local #48, started the Wage Earner's Suffrage League in the city. Minna O'Donnell joined LaRue in leadership of the League. When Maud Younger became the third side of this triangle, she brought the middle class suffragists and the working class women together on behalf of suffrage. The League's action likely led to the precious few majority votes women won in the precincts of the working class neighborhoods of San Francisco.

Why Wage-Earning
Women Should Vote

By Maud Younger.

More than seven million women in the United States daily leave their homes to go out in the world and fight beside men for their living. They work under greater disadvantages and temptations than men, they work for longer hours and lower wages, they bear the greater burdens of our industrial system, yet they have not the protection which men have of the ballot.

Good laws are even more necessary to the woman, for she is the mother of the next generation, and upon the conditions under which she works depends largely the health of herself and of her children. The stunted growth and impaired vitality of the English working people to-day are the direct results of lack of legislation in their behalf when the introduction of machinery made possible the great exploitation of labor.

It is of the utmost importance that there should be **good factory laws,** that a woman should work under sanitary conditions with protection for life and limb, that she should not work long hours, nor late at night, etc. Yet she has no representatives to make or enforce the laws so necessary to her and the community.

The women of California are in daily competition with Asiatics. They have a constant struggle to maintain wages and conditions under which white women can work and live. Yet, the native-born Chinese have a weapon far more powerful than any that she has. They can vote for the law-makers who govern her, and she cannot.

The working women of California have gained everything themselves, inch by inch, through the **Union.** Without a voice in the government, they turn to the Union for protection. They give it their allegiance. But the Union cannot do everything. They need good laws to protect them at home as well as at work. And they need good laws far more than the rich. If food is impure, trust prices exorbitant, dwelling houses unsanitary, public schools bad, public hospitals poor, street cars abominable, police protection inadequate, the rich can pay for private service. The poor have no choice.

All these things directly concern women. Her home, her children, are her especial province, yet she cannot demand the laws necessary for their protection.

There are two ways to secure laws—by **vote** and by **"influence."** Wage-earners cannot afford "influence." They must elect men who will pass and enforce the laws they need. Legislation in the interests of the working class does not come unless they demand it. An appeal to the courtesy of legislators is never so effective as a demand backed up by votes. The workingman's vote looms large and threatening on the politician's horizon. The woman's vote is necessary to secure the woman's interests. Even in the labor movement, where women are probably treated with greater courtesy than elsewhere, they find that

Maud Younger (1870-1936)

As a San Francisco socialite for her first thirty years, Maud Younger could have lived comfortably. A chance, almost quirky twist, changed her life forever. Going through New York City on the way to Paris to visit her father, she decided to "see the slums" and stopped at the College Settlement. That "tour of the slums" took five years. She emerged as a radical, an organizer, and a champion for the working woman. In New York she became a waitress and concluded that waitresses must be organized, unionized, and protective legislation for them must be passed.

In San Francisco, in 1908, she pioneered a waitresses union, became president of the local, and served for three terms as delegate to the Central Trades and Labor Council. She advocated the amendment for the eight-hour workday for women. The amendment along with women's right to vote, passed on October 10, 1911. Having won suffrage in California, she joined the national campaign for the Nineteenth Amendment in Washington, D.C.

Although she was a petite woman, she possessed an impressive oratory. She gave the keynote speech to the founding of Alice Paul's National Woman's Party, and the memorial oration for Inez Milhoulland Boissevan's funeral in Washington, D.C. She became the spokesperson for the National Woman's Party, and toured America declaring the mandate of the Party. In step with Alice Paul's confrontational style, Maud Younger organized demonstrations, public meetings and pressured politicians by directing constituents to demand the Nineteenth Amendment from Congressmen. A powerful voice and a spirited leader.

they must constantly look after their own interests. Working women are the backbone of the English suffrage movement today.

Formerly women did not have separate interests. Everything now made in the factory was then made in the home. There materials were woven, clothes, rugs, candles, soap, matches, butter, cheese, etc., etc., were made. There women did the work. They did not come in contact with the outside world nor share its responsibilities. That was left to the men, and men made the laws to protect their own interests. Women had none. They were not even tax-payers. Everything they had belonged to their husbands. A man could even will away his unborn child. But when the introduction of machinery removed work to the factories, women were forced to follow. They no longer made at home the things they needed; they had to go out into the world and earn the money with which to buy them. The status of women was entirely changed.

The form of any government and society depends upon **economic conditions.** A change in industrial life brings a change in laws and customs. Conditions under which women work and live are constantly changing and laws must be changed to meet them. Women are now in daily contact with the world; they do their work in the world and share its responsibilities with men. It is not their choice. It has been forced upon them. The proportion of self-supporting women is rapidly increasing. **Self-protection requires that they should vote. Progress demands it.**

The grounds on which men have obtained an extension of the franchise are: 1—Government must rest on the consent of the governed; 2—Taxation without representation is tyranny. These arguments apply equally to women. There can be **no democracy** where half the population is governed without its consent.

It is said that all the women will not vote. Well, neither do all men. But it would be unjust to disfranchise all men because a portion of them do not use the ballot.

It is said that "women's sphere is in the **home,**" but this does not apply to the seven million women in America who must leave their homes in order to live. Besides, no woman can keep her home pure in evil surroundings. **A corrupt city taints every home in it.** Where women vote, the home-loving women are among the strongest advocates of suffrage. And this has not been found to make them less womanly.

Women now vote in **New Zealand, Australia, Tasmania, Norway, Finland and Isle of Man.** They have municipal suffrage in **England, Iceland, Scotland, Wales, Canada, Sweden, Denmark and Natal.** In England they vote for everything except parliament. In Finland more than twenty women are members of parliament. In five of the United States women have equal suffrage with men; in more than twenty others, partial suffrage.

In different parts of the country the vote has been given to negroes, Indians, Hindoos and other Asiatics. Have they greater interests to protect than have the American women? Are they more capable of citizenship

In California every adult may vote excepting only Mongolians, Indians, idiots, insane, criminals and women.

The country is looking to California as the next State to get the ballot. It is not a question of the indefinite future. The suffrage amendment has passed the legislature by a large majority in both houses. The question is before the voters.

"California Next"

Votes for Mothers

**Politics governs
even the purity of the
milk supply.
It is not outside the home**

but

inside
the
baby

Charlotte
Perkins
Gilman

When the great intellectual and feminist Charlotte Perkins Gilman (1860-1935) settled in the Bay Area in the late 1890s, her book, *Woman and Economics* (1898) was already on her mind. One might say her experiences in California furnished her with the inspiration to write this book, which redefined woman's role in the home and in society. In addition to organizing the Woman's Congresses, Mrs. Gilman also wrote flyers as well as poems for the 1896 and 1911 campaigns. This handout is an example of her work.

Phil Rader (*San Francisco Bulletin*, March 26, 1910) poked good naturedly at this burning, profound question: food or the vote?

The Call Has the Best
COMMERCIAL
THEATRICAL
REAL ESTATE
SPORTING
SOCIETY
MARINE

NEWS

THE *San Francisco* CALL

THE WEATHER
YESTERDAY — Highest temperature, 56;
lowest Friday night, 50.
FORECAST FOR TODAY—Fair with
fog in the morning and at night; light south
wind, changing to brisk west.

VOLUME CX.—NO. 67.   SEVENTY-SIX PAGES—SAN FRANCISCO, SUNDAY, AUGUST 6, 1911.—PAGES 37 TO 48.   PRICE FIVE CENTS.

Hereby The Call Pledges Its Aggressive Support to the Political Emancipation of California's Women

John D. Spreckels, the eldest son of the famous sugar millionaire Claus Spreckels, was the editor of *The Call*, which not only advocated women's suffrage, but provided a worthy historical trail of the activities of the women's suffrage campaign of 1911. *The Call* distinguished itself as distinctly separate from the liquor establishment in San Francisco when it declared its aggressive support for suffrage on the front page of the Sunday edition, August 6, 1911.

When *The Call* could have asked its colleagues to "eat crow."

After the October 10, 1911 election, when both leading San Francisco papers, the *Examiner* and *Chronicle*, declared suffrage dead again, *The Call* reminded everybody that all the votes were not yet counted. Actually, *The Call* predicted that suffrage would win by 4,000 votes! The final margin was 3,587. In this article, *The Call* pointed out how the rest of the San Francisco papers were wrong and only it was right. So it was. Good reporting.

SUFFRAGE AUTO PARADE

One of the most impressive and inspiring sights that Berkeley has seen for many a moon will be the suffrage automobile parade that will cover the main thoroughfares of the city Friday evening. Headed by a brass band playing patriotic airs, 50 machines, gay with yellow streamers, yellow banners bearing the "strange device" SUFFRAGE FOR WOMEN, and other equally pertinent mottoes, will leave the Hotel Shattuck at 7 o'clock and wend its joyous way through enthusiastic crowds. The procession will halt at prominent corners and addresses will be made by well-known speakers. Among those secured to speak are Prof. E. O. James, Mrs. E. S. Watson, president of the state league; Albert Elliott, P. M. Fisher and Mrs. Blum. The latter two were among the speakers in Sacramento during the state fair, and created a great deal of enthusiasm. Mrs. Katherine Waugh McCullock will also be among the speakers.

Among those who will occupy automobiles in the parade are Mrs. Harland, Mrs. Wm. Keith, Mrs. F. F. Bunker, Mrs. Aaron Schloss, Mrs. C. C. Hall, Mr. and Mrs. N. Cleaveland and guests, Mr. and Mrs. C. F. Weiland and guests, Dr. and Mrs. Chas. Elliott, Warren Cheney Co. automobile with guests, Miss Leola Hall and guests, Mr. and Mrs. Claude Gegnoux and guests, Mr. and Mrs. Chas. Camm and guests, Mrs. Elizabeth Witter, Mr. and Mrs. L. E. Blochman and guests, Mr. and Mrs. John Nicol and guests, Miss Hayward. Mr. and Mrs. Fred C. Schram of Richmond with several machines filled with guests Mrs. Elinor Carlisle, Mr. and Mrs. Mosher, Mr. and Mrs. Samuel C. Haight, Dr. and Mrs. W. F. Southard, Mr. and Mrs. Walter Brown, Mrs. Ella Moore, Mr. and Mrs. S. J. Bens, Mrs. Irving Scott, Jr., Dr. and Mrs. John Snook, Mr. and Mrs. Perry Thompkins, Mr. and Mrs. H. H. Sherwood and Mrs. Holmes. There are many others planning to enter the parade, not only Berkeley folk but people from all the bay cities. Anyone wishing to join this "procession of progress" or lend a machine to the cause, call upon Mrs. Harland.

The parade will start from Hotel Shattuck at 7:30, proceed north on Shattuck to University, countermarch on Shattuck to Center, where speeches will be made, then down Shattuck to where the avenue crosses Adeline, south on Adeline to Alcatraz, where more speeches will be made, then west to San Pablo, north on San Pablo to University, another speaking point, eastward on University to Shattuck, southward on Shattuck to Bancroft, eastward on Bancroft to Telegraph, where the last halt will be made.

At each of the speaking points the addresses will be continuous, one speaker following the preceding one, who will move on to the next point. In this way everybody will have the opportunity to hear all the prominent men and women who are to give the addresses without the inconvenience of following the long line of march. It will also prevent congestion of traffic.

MAYOR WILSON TO TALK

Mayor Wilson is an exceedingly busy man these days. Taking an active interest in the suffrage campaign and being an eloquent speaker, he is in great demand not only around the bay, but Los Angeles has telegraphed repeatedly for him to talk there. The last invitation was to address an audience of 5,000 next Monday night, but previous engagement to talk here made him refuse. This will be on the evening before election day at the High school auditorium. Miss Fannie McLean, who has been talking throughout the state, has also reserved her services for her home town this last evening, and will be among the speakers at the final rally. Mayor Wilson spoke three times last evening in different parts of San Francisco. He was hurried from one point to another in an automobile, and several thousand people heard his eloquent addresses.

TOUR FACTORY SECTION

Mrs. Hester Harland, with Rev. Florence Buck of Alameda and Mrs. Robert A. Dean of San Francisco, made a tour of the manufacturing district in West Berkeley at noon today and addressed a large number of enthusiastic workers on the suffrage amendment.

The open roadster became the stellar mascot of the 1911 campaign. The College Equal Suffrage League had a special car, a blue one, which members named the Blue Liner. It became their signature, their pet, their main way to tour California and spread the suffrage word. The use of the car, a new, flashy device on the California scene, was a brilliant public relations touch. Not only did it serve as "wheels," but also it was a place from which to speak, and it was especially appealing to men—the people who would vote for the suffrage amendment. Trimmed like a pet horse, the car sported yellow streamers, and proudly carried the suffragists throughout California.

Ode to the Farmers who Voted a Majority for Us

Out of the dust of the street
Came the demise;
Out of the fumes of the clubs,
Scorn of our trial.

But from the strength of the hills
Men's voices hailed us;
God bless our farmer-folk,
Scarce a man failed us!

This is how the College Equal Suffrage League explained the victory for suffrage.

March 28, 1912, heralded an historic first action for the women of California: This was the first time in their lives they could vote! Left to right: Elizabeth Gerberding, Mary Sperry and Nellie Eyster pose for the camera. S.F. Voter Registrar Zemansky appointed women to fill one half the number of precinct positions. May 14 was the first presidential primary in the state and the first opportunity for women to partici-pate in national politics.

The Road to Washington
1915

POLITICAL FLIRTATION

Uncle Sam Flirting With the Susan B. Anthony and the Shafroth amendments. He really prefers the simple maid, who dances so well, Miss Shafroth, for all her expensive ruffles.

Drawn by Nina E. Allender

In 1914, Senator John F. Shafroth (Colorado), proposed a suffrage amendment (S-3507) that would give women the right to vote only for a member of the House of Representatives or the Senate. At the Panama-Pacific Exposition (1915), women at the Suffrage Union proceedings debated the merits of the Shafroth and Susan B. Anthony amendments. Words were hot, arguments were heated, but in the end the women of the Suffrage Union pledged to support Susan B. Anthony. This cartoon depicts the final decision of the radical woman as partner to Uncle Sam. Imagine Susan B. Anthony dancing with Uncle Sam!

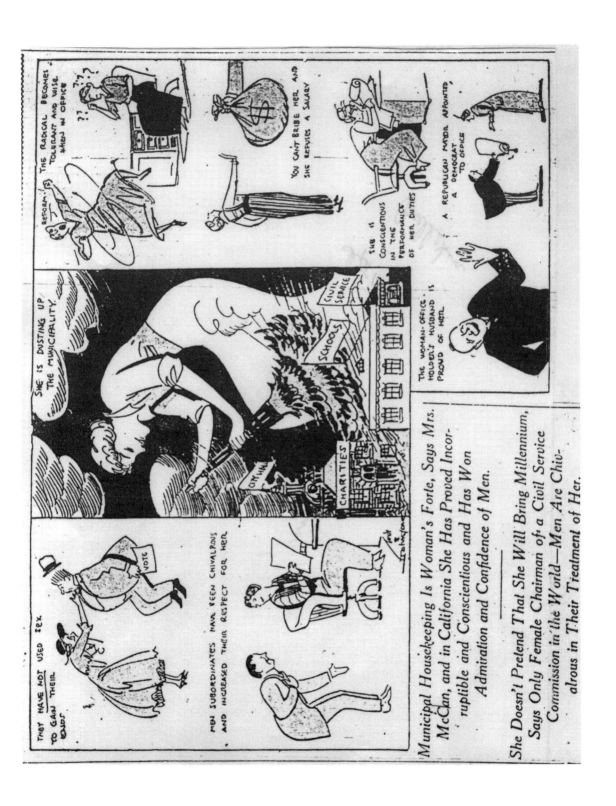

Municipal Housekeeping Is Woman's Forte, Says Mrs. McClan, and in California She Has Proved Incorruptible and Conscientious and Has Won Admiration and Confidence of Men.

She Doesn't Pretend That She Will Bring Millennium, Says Only Female Chairman of a Civil Service Commission in the World—Men Are Chivalrous in Their Treatment of Her.

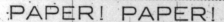

PAPER! PAPER!

Miss Ruth White, One of the Many Suffragists Selling the Belmont Edition of The Bulletin Today

EAST GREETS EDITORS OF SUFFRAGE BULLETIN

(Special Dispatch to The Bulletin.)

NEW YORK, Sept. 18.—The Empire State Suffrage Campaign Committee, Mrs. Carrie Chapman Catt, chairman, today extended greetings to the women voters of the West, represented by suffragists who today edited the San Francisco Bulletin.

"The committee welcomes every effort such as the women are making in San Francisco today," said Mrs. Catt, "and extends greetings to the enfranchised women of the Pacific Coast. It hopes that the women of New York will be included among the enfranchised after November 2, and trusts that the women voters of the West will not forget the struggle that is on in the East."

(Special Dispatch to The Bulletin.)

LOS ANGELES, Sept. 18.—Great interest was displayed today by Mrs. Estelle Lawton Lindsey, City Councilwoman and former acting Mayor, when she learned that the San Francisco Bulletin was being edited by Mrs. O. H. P. Belmont with a staff of women. Mrs. Lindsey said:

"If I were in Mrs. Belmont's position today and able to dictate the policy of a metropolitan publica-

This Edition

Today's issue of The Bulletin is devoted to the issue of nation-wide votes for women. It is edited by Mrs. O. H. P. Belmont, assisted by Sara Bard Field of Portland, Ore., managing editor; Alice Paul of Washington, D. C., news editor; Doris Stevens of New York, city editor; Mrs. William Kent, wife of Congressman Kent of California, telegraph editor, and Mrs.

MRS. BELMONT TO EDIT THE BULLETIN ON SATURDAY

Leader in Suffrage Cause to Conduct Journal for Day

Silhouette of Mrs. Belmont, Made by Beatrix Sherman in the Palace of Food Products at the Fair.

Mrs. O. H. P. Belmont, best known of the many eminent woman leaders in the fight for equal suffrage, will edit The Bulletin next Saturday. For one day she will be in complete charge of the policy of the paper and can write and print what she pleases.

The editorial staff for the great issue will include many of the brilliant women now here attending the Women Voters' Convention, a gathering of historic importance which has as its object the furtherance of the campaign for the Susan B. Anthony amendment to the Federal Constitution.

Mrs. Belmont is the national chairman of the Congressional Union for Woman Suffrage and is a tower of strength to the cause for which she is battling. Her contributions and supervision, with articles by other famous women, will make this special edition a memorable number of The Bulletin.

Alva E. Belmont

Verse by Suffragist Decrys Attitude of Woman From Boston Town

By BERTHA MONROE RICKOFF

BALLAD OF A SUFFRAGETTE

There's a lady and we greet her, who is paid to
come from Boston
To teach the California suffragette
How to learn to be a lady; that the land pays
all the taxes,
And that man's the greatest moral factor yet.

We have many points in common with this in-
teresting anti,
We acknowledge that we rather like the men;
We believe in wine for dinner and we often
serve a cocktail,
And we think the needle mightier than the pen.

But the quite old fashioned anti thinks that
every man is perfect;
That a voter is a brilliant, blazing star—
While the suffragette is modern; she deplores
their peccadillos,
But she likes the brutal tyrants as they are!

Oh, you quaint and sleeping antis holding deeds
to lots and houses
And believing things are ever as they seem,
Get awake, it is October, and the bills are at the
courthouse,
For the land that pays the taxes is a dream!

You go home to cold old Boston where the east
wind cuts the heartstrings,
Leave us where the calla blossoms on the
ground;
We can rear our homes and children, cheer our
men and clean our cities,
And we need not learn from Boston to be
sound.

There's a grander type of women than New
England ever nurtured,
Though lofty types your early years could
boast;
There's a sweeter task for ladies than to be
aristocratic,
And there's something on the free Pacific
coast

That shall make the whole world better when
the fair shall call it hither,
And the eastern states shall travel home
again,
With the lesson of our progress, the example of
our women,
And the state that called them equal with its
men.

It's woman this, and woman that, and woman go away. But "it's please deliver, madam," when there's Income Tax to pay.

SONG OF FREE WOMEN

Tune—"Marseillaise"   Words by—Sara Bard Field

First Chorus.

> Hark! what hosts, white-robed, advancing
> Through Night's dark portal to the Dawn?
> What might purpose in the glancing?
> What vision look they far upon?
> What vision look they far upon?

Second Chorus.

> We are women clad in new power.
> We see the weak. We hear their plea.
> We march to set our sisters free.
> Lo! has rung the chime from Freedom's tower.

All.

> We come. We come at last.
> Night's portal we have past.
> We come. We come. Trust thou our might.
> Thou, too, shall walk in Light.

First Chorus.

> On they come nor know retreating;
> Eastward from the West they move,
> Souls upon the Morning beating,
> Womanhood made one in love.
> Womanhood made one in love.

Second Chorus.

> No more we bend the knee imploring.
> No longer urge our cause with tears.
> We have rent asunder binding fears.
> We are women strong for women warring.

All.

> We come. We come at last.
> Nights' portal we have passed.
> We come. We come. Trust thou our might.
> Thou, too, shall walk in Light.

Words written for the Woman Voters' Demonstration given in the Court of
Abundance, Panama-Pacific International Exposition, September 16, 1915.

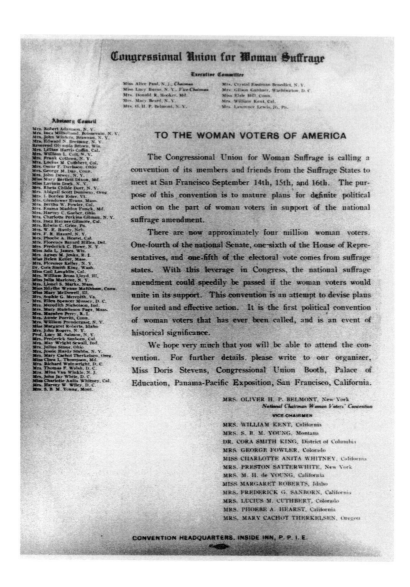

California and Washington, D.C. had a special relationship since the early days when Senator Aaron Sargent and Ellen Clark Sargent began their suffrage work representing California while living in Washington. After California women won their vote in 1911, some of their leaders continued the national suffrage campaign by moving to Washington. Alice Parks, Maud Younger and Anita Whitney joined Mrs. Kent in the nation's capital working for the passage of the Nineteenth Amendment.

The successful 1911 suffrage campaign in the state gave four million California women the right to vote. Four million new voters raised the specter of considerable political clout in the eyes of politicians in Washington. One example of this political power was the proceedings of the Woman Voters Convention (September 14, 15 and 16) of the Congressional Union for Woman Suffrage at the Panama-Pacific Exposition, which, in San Francisco in 1915, was the first convention of women voters in the history of the United States. National activists like Alice Paul saw the potential of a public relations event promoting the national suffrage amendment still unresolved. While under the skies of San Francisco, the Voters Convention connected California to Washington, D.C. Representatives and the Governors of suffrage states attended and spoke. Women from China, Italy and Persia attended and spoke. National suffrage politicians from all over the United States attended and spoke. They joined the local and state political women in this historic event marking the advance of the women's vote in America. The grand finale, on Friday evening of September 16, 1915, sent a motor car with four women and a petition to Congress and the President on the road to Washington, D.C.

Alice Paul (1885-1977)

Alice Paul, a Quaker social worker from New Jersey, became the brave and brilliant head of the Woman's Political Party. She was responsible for the cunning political tactic of using the potential power of California women voters by holding both political parties responsible for passing the Nineteenth Amendment. If congressional representatives did not press the Nineteenth Amendment forward, she would warn those politicians that they could be voted out of office. At a signal from her, California women voters would press their local politicians with phone calls and office visits. Men understood that power tactic and conceded.

At the Court of Abundance of the Panama-Pacific Exposition (1915) in San Francisco, she spoke at the closing ceremony of the first convention of American women voters, September 14, 15 and 16. Typical of her talent to make a point dramatically, Miss Paul conceived the event that proceeded from the Court of Abundance, out the gates of the Exposition and across the country to Washington, D.C. It was farewell to the envoys, Sara Bard Field and Frances Jolliffe, in a roadster loaned and driven by two Swedish women, Misses Kindstedt and Kindberg. They carried a petition pressing for the Nineteenth Amendment to President Woodrow Wilson.

Just as women caught on to the bicycle in the last years of the nineteenth century, women took to the automobile in the twentieth. Not only driving, women also learned the basic mechanics of successful car-keeping such as changing oil. The Willys-Overland had a good reputation, and its originating company eventually produced Jeeps in the later part of the twentieth century. Any journey by car, even today, takes a certain spirited attitude to make it happen. Needless to say, four women traversing roads hardly there, always seeking gas not easily found, accomplished a task worthy of the triumphant parade they received down Pennsylvania Avenue on the road to the White House in 1915!

Congressional Union for Woman Suffrage

According to the *San Francisco Bulletin*, on a Thursday night, September 16, 1915, at the Court of Abundance in the Panama Pacific Exposition, so ended "...the most dramatic and significant suffrage convention that has probably ever been held in the history of the world." Picture a crowd of 10,000 attending these closing ceremonies filled with symbols of suffrage and feminism. In the large arch framing the base of the court tower hung a banner reading, "We demand an amendment to the Constitution of the United States enfranchising women." Choruses sang "The March of the Women," and "Song of Free Women," words composed by Sara Bard Field, to the music of "The Marsellaise." Energy heightened as the crowd joined in singing. This final action of the Congressional Union for Woman Suffrage sent two elected delegates, Frances Jolliffe and Sara Bard Field, to Washington. Sara Bard Field held the petition signed by Exposition visitors. It contained 600,000 names and would be circulated for more names among the cities along the road to Washington, D.C. As the *Bulletin* related:

> "Then all at once the great brightly-colored picture and its dark background began to disintegrate and fade. The court darkened, but colorful masses of women were forming in procession to escort the envoys to the gates of the Exposition. Orange lanterns swayed in the breeze, purple, white and gold draperies fluttered, the blare of the band burst forth, and the great surging crowd followed to the gates.
>
> There Miss Ingebore Kindstedt and Miss A. M. Kindberg of Providence, Rhode Island, who have purchased the car that is to take the crusaders on their long journey, met the solemn procession. The Overland car was covered with suffrage streamers. Miss Kindberg was at the wheel. To the wild cheering of the crowd Miss Jolliffe and Mrs. Field, the two envoys for Washington, were seated. The crowd surged close with final messages. Cheers burst forth as the gates opened and the big car swung through, ending the most dramatic and significant suffrage convention that has probably ever been held in the history of the world."

The Court of Abundance (at night), Panama-Pacific International Exposition, 1915

THE MARCH OF THE WOMEN.

ETHEL SMYTH, Mus. Doc.

PIANO.

2

Long, long—we in the past
  Covered in dread from the light of heaven,
Strong, strong—stand we at last,
  Fearless in faith and with sight new-given.
Strength with its beauty, Life with its duty.
  (Hear the voice, oh hear and obey!)
These, these—beckon us on!
  Open your eyes to the blaze of day.

3

Comrades—ye who have dared!
  First in the battle to strive and sorrow!
Scorned, spurned—naught have ye cared,
  Raising your eyes to a wider morrow.
Ways that are weary, days that are dreary,
  Toil and pain by faith ye have borne;
Hail, hail—victors ye stand,
  Wearing the wreath that the brave have worn!

4

Life, strife—these two are one,
  Naught can ye win but by faith and daring.
On, on—that ye have done
  But for the work of to-day preparing.
Firm in reliance, laugh a defiance,
  (Laugh in hope, for sure is the end.)
March, march—many as one,
  Shoulder to shoulder and friend to friend.

Courtesy of the San Francisco "BULLETIN"

Trail of Light (timeline)

1854   Sarah M. Pellet, M.D. mounted the lectern and spoke about equality of women, San Francisco.

1858   A new women's literary magazine, *The Hesperian*, launched by editor Mrs. A. M. Schulz, eventually replaced in 1863 by Elizabeth Schenck.

1863   Lisle Lester promoted women's rights as editor of the *Pacific Monthly*.

1867   *Banner of Progress*, a weekly Spiritualist newspaper, published news about the women's movement.

1868   Women's Cooperative Printing Union organized by Agnes Peterson.

1868   February 18, Laura deForce Gordon gave a speech, that launched the suffrage movement in San Francisco.

1869   Testing the validity of the Fourteenth and Fifteenth Constitutional amendments including women's franchise, a statewide petition was presented to the state legislature to secure the vote for California women.

1869   July patriots formed the nucleus group from which the state suffrage association formed.

1870   The founding of the California Woman Suffrage Association. Sarah Wallis, first president.

1870   Emily Pitts Stevens bought the *Sunday Mercury*, changed the name to *Saturday Evening Mercury*, the first women's suffrage publication in the West. Name changed to the *Pioneer,* with the same pro-suffrage stance.

1871   Susan B. Anthony and Elizabeth C. Stanton visited San Francisco and the Bay Area. Susan B. Anthony toured the West Coast and returned to San Francisco (August-December).

1871   The trial: Mrs. Van Valkenburg sued the Santa Cruz registrar of voters, Mr. Brown, for refusing her request to register to vote. Her case defeated. Appeal lost.

1871   Laura deForce Gordon, as a member of the Independent Party, San Joaquin County, ran for the state senate.

1872   Emily Pitts Stevens founded the Woman's Publishing Co. promoting women's work as typesetters.

1872   Nellie C. Tator applied to Santa Cruz Court for admission to the bar. Denied.

1874   Pro-suffrage weekly Spiritualist journal *Common Sense*, edited by Amanda and William Slocum, ran for one year.

1876   Marietta Beers-Stow published *Probate Confiscation*, a scathing account of the horrors for widows and children in the Probate Court.

1878   Through efforts of Clara S. Foltz, the Woman Lawyers' Bill signed into law, giving women the right to practice law in California.

1878   First words about suffrage uttered in Congress by the Senator from California, Aaron A. Sargent (Nevada City). Amendment proposed.

1879   Clara Shortridge Foltz and Laura deForce Gordon argued in the Fourth District Court on behalf of Foltz's suit against Hastings School of the Law for denying women admission to Hastings. Case won.

1880   In running for the San Francisco Board of Education, Marietta Beers-Stow organized a political rally at her home, reportedly the first rally of this kind.

1881   *The Woman's Herald of Industry and Social Science Cooperator* founder Marietta Beers-Stow championed children's and women's rights. She proclaimed her paper as the only one in America entirely edited by women, who did all mechanical work except the press.

1881   Mary McHenry Keith was the first woman graduate of Hastings School of the Law.

1882   As an independent, Marietta Beers-Stow was the first woman to run for governor of the state.

1884   Belva Lockwood (attorney from Washington, D.C.) ran for President of the United States with Marietta Beers-Stow as her running-mate. They were nominated by a convention held in San Francisco and led by Clara Foltz, Marietta Beers-Stow and Drs. Hall and Corbett.

1887   The Sketch Club, the first women's artists club in California, founded in San Francisco. Still functioning as the San Francisco Woman Artists Association, 370 Hayes Street.

1888   The Century Club, San Francisco's first women's club, founded. Still flourishing at 1355 Franklin Street.

1893   At the Chicago Columbian Fair, the remarkable Woman's Congress attracted huge audiences, second only in popular attendance to the World's Parliament of Religions.

1894   The Pacific Coast Woman's Congress Association held its first of four years of congresses in San Francisco.

1895   Susan B. Anthony came to San Francisco to prepare for the 1896 campaign to amend the state constitution to give women the right to vote.

1896   The arrival of the national team from Washington, D.C. to join with the locals to run the suffrage campaign of 1896.

1896   The amendment to give California women the right to vote was defeated, November 3.

1897   The California Club, a women's civic organization, founded in San Francisco. Still exists on Clay Street.

1906   From the Presidio in San Francisco, at her own expense, Catharine Reed Balentine published *The Yellow Ribbon*, the official paper of the West Coast suffrage societies.

1906   A very successful suffrage convention was held in San Francisco amidst the ashes and rubble of the fire and earthquake.

1908   In Oakland, California, Lillian Harris Coffin organized and led a march of 300 suffragists to the Republican state convention.

1910   Selina Solomons founded the Votes-for-Women Club in downtown San Francisco.

1910   Led by Selina Solomons, Votes-for-Women members confronted the San Francisco registrar of voters with their request to register to vote. Denied.

1911   The California women's campaign to go for the vote began six months before the Oct. 10 election.

1911   By a slim margin of 3,587 votes, California women won their right to vote with the passage of an amendment to the state constitution. The Sixth Star was won.

1912   Selina Solomons' book, *How We Won the Vote in 1911,* published in San Francisco.

1915   Convened at the Panama-Pacific Exposition in San Francisco, the first meeting of American women voters. A massive petition pressing the Nineteenth Constitutional Amendment was dispatched by car to the nation's capital.

1919   California Governor Stephens convened a special session of the legislature to ratify the Nineteenth Amendment.

1920   August 26 was the final adoption of the Nineteenth Amendment.

THE YEAR OF THE VOTING WOMAN HAD ARRIVED IN AMERICA.

Writing Notes

I am as expansive as I am opinionated here in documenting sources about the California suffrage campaigns. Since so little has been published about these elections, I feel responsible to reveal my paths of search to lessen the work of subsequent researchers, hopefully to show how accessible the material is, and to share my enthusiasm of the discovery.

Because the stars of the National Woman Suffrage Association came to California to help in both campaigns, their stories become part of California's story. Also the reverse of that became true. Namely, once Western women won the right to vote, these National stars, such as Alice Paul and Carrie Chapman Catt, used the power of that Western vote—particularly that of populous California—to influence the passage of the Nineteenth Amendment. I began my research by reading these sources for their background information, as well as an introduction to the national suffrage stars and their response to the Western women's vote when it was won.

Adams, Mildred. *The Right to be People*. (N.Y., 1967)

Banner, Lois W. *Elizabeth Cady Stanton*. (Mass., 1980)

Catt, Carrie Chapman. *Woman Suffrage and Politics*. (N.Y., 1923)

Evans, Sara M. *Born for Liberty*. (N.Y., 1989)

Fowler, Robert Booth. *Carrie Catt*. (Mass., 1986)

Flexner, Eleanor. *Century of Struggle*. (N.Y., 1972)

Frost, Elizabeth and Cullen-Dupont, Kathryn. *Woman's Suffrage in America* (N.Y., 1992)

Griffith, Elizabeth. *In Her Own Right*. (N.Y., 1984)

Grimes, Alan P. *The Puritan Ethic and Woman Suffrage*. (Conn., 1980)

Harper, Ida Husted. *The Life and Work of Susan B. Anthony*. (Indiana, 1908)

Irwin, Inez Harper. *The Story of the Woman's Party*. (N.Y., 1921)

Notable American Women, 1607-1950. Vols. 1-3. Mass. 1971

Scott, Andrew W. and Anne Firor. *One Half the People: The Fight for Woman Suffrage*.(Ill., 1982)

Sherr, Lynn. *Failure is Impossible*. (N.Y., 1995)

Stanton, Elizabeth Cady. *Eighty Years and More Remeniscences*. 1815-1897. (N.Y., 1992 reprint)

Stevens, Doris. *Jailed For Freedom*. (N.Y., 1920)

For the California story these were indispensible:

Beeton, Beverly. *Woman Vote in the West: The Woman Suffrage Movement 1869-1896*. (N.Y., 1986)

Davis, Reda. *California Women: A Guide to their Politics (1885-1911)*. (Cal., 1967)

Solomons, Selina. *How We Won the Vote in California*. (Cal., 1912)

Rodes, Donald Waller. "The California Woman Suffrage Campaign of 1911." Master's Thesis, (unpublished., 1974)

The Bancroft Library in Berkeley has boxes of material on women's suffrage in California; about the College Equal Suffrage League; copies of *The Yellow Ribbon* and *The Western Woman*; the Ponds/McHenry/Keith papers, rich and full of memorabilia, letters, notes, clippings and pictures. Selina Solomons' papers do not reveal as much about her as Shirley Sargent's *Solomons of the Sierra* (Flying Spur Press, 1990) and Irena Narell's article "Jewish Women Pioneers in California History," *Na'Amat Woman*, May-June, 1987; as well as her *Our*

City (California, 1981)

Newspaper accounts of suffrage activities and events were as indispensible as they were revealing about the newspapers themselves. Michael deYoung's anti-anything new-woman bias soon became very clear. The *Chronicle* rarely covered a suffrage situation sympathetically, if at all. For evenhanded suffrage and new-woman stories, Hearst's *Examiner* and *The Call*, owned at one time by Clara Shortridge Foltz's brother, Charles, proved valuable. For stories about each campaign, I read papers dated before, during and after the elections, political conventions, and any suffrage stars' events.

The 1896 San Francisco voting records were destroyed by the 1906 fires. To locate court cases, I used the Law Library of City Hall and Hastings School of the Law, San Francisco.

Background reading for the politics of San Francisco, the following were helpful:

Bean, Walton. *California*. (N.Y., 1973)
Caughey, John. *California*. (N.J., 1964)
Cleland, Robert Glass. *Wilderness to Empire*. (N.Y., 1959)
Issel, William and Cherny, Robert. *San Francisco 1865-1932*. (Cal., 1986)

For the story of Senator Aaron Sargent and Ellen Clark Sargent, see Marion Tingley's "A Quest for Rights: Woman Suffragists", *Sierra Heritage*, January and February, 1992.

Woman's Congress material is part of the Ponds/McHenry/Keith papers. Discussions about the Woman's Congress at the Chicago Columbian Fair, appear in Jeanne M. Weimann's *The Fair Women* (Chicago, 1981)

G. Thomas Edwards' *Sowing Good Seeds* (Oregon, 1990) followed Susan B. Anthony on her trip up the Pacific Coast to Washington and back in 1871. Ida Husted Harper's indisputable volumes, *The Life and Work of Susan B. Anthony*, contain her trips to California including, 1895-96.

Material on Santa Cruz's feminist, Georgiana Bruce Kirby can be found in *Georgiana B. Kirby: Feminist Reformer of the West*, Santa Cruz Historical Society, 1987.

Information about Laura deForce Gordon can be found in the *Notable American Women*, Vol. 2 and *Pen Portraits*, R.R. Parkinson (S.F., 1878)

See the Sarah B. Cooper story in *Notable American Women*, Vol. 1, and the *San Francisco Chronicle*, December 12, 1896.

The Leila and Mary Curtis (Richardson) story is from the *WPA Art Research*, Vol. 5, under Mary Curtis Richardson; also David A. McGibney's 1987 Master's Thesis at Mills, "Mary Curtis Richardson: An American Woman Artist."

Roger Levenson's *Women Printers in Northern California* (Santa Barbara, 1994), shows the close relationship between printing, publishing, writing, Spiritualism, and suffrage in San Francisco. Levenson's coverage of Emily Pitts Stevens' involvement in early suffrage in San Francisco is worthy, as well as Dr. Robert Chandler's article in *California History*, "In the Van: Spiritualists as Catalysts for the California Women's Suffrage Movement" (Fall, 1994) *Astrea*, by Mrs. Thorndike, is in the San Francisco Main Library, sixth floor.

To read pages and pages about liquor establishments in San Francisco and other towns in California in the late 1890s, try the 1893 *Gazeteer*. Figures of the 1896 election were gleaned from newspapers, particulary the *Examiner* and *The Call*.

For discussion about the advent and impact of the Lincoln-Roosevelt League in California, I suggest: J. Gregg Lyne, "The Lincoln-Roosevelt League," *Historical Society of Southern California Quarterly*, XXV, Sept. 1943, and Bean, Caughey, Issel and Cherney, and Cleland. College Equal Suffrage League material have their own box at the Bancroft. *Winning Equal*

Suffrage in California (1912) includes reports of the College Equal Suffrage League of Northern California, especially recounts of the famous Blue Liner campaign roadster. The Hester Harland papers about suffrage cover both 1896 and 1911 with newspaper clippings and other ephemera. In *How We Won the Vote in California*, Selina Solomons documented the 1911 campaign with an inimitable savvy and sassiness that showed her feisty personality.

Clara Shortridge Foltz's papers do not exist but she wrote her autobiography in her publication, *The New American Woman*, dates April 1916 to June 1918. Useful information about her life is in *Hastings' Law Journal*, Vol. 27, November 1979, "Clara Shortridge Foltz: Pioneer in the Law," by Mortimer D. Schwartz, Susan L. Brandt and Patience Milrod. Also *Notable American Women* Vol I., and *Hastings College of the Law* by Thomas Gordon Barnes, (Cal., 1978)

At the California Historical Society, Mm. Louise Agatha Josephine Bacon Sorbier's papers and scrapbooks are especially helpful about the Woman's Congresses in California. Mm. Sorbier was on the Board of Directors of the Woman's Congress.

The registrar of voters records of the September, October and November 1911 elections in San Francisco county exist through the Koshland History Center, 6th floor of the San Francisco Main Library, Civic Center.

Regarding coverage of the Wage Earner's League's involvement in the 1911 campaign, see Sue Englander's unpublished paper, "Organizing for Woman Suffrage in Labor's City: The Wage Earner's League's Unique Role in the 1911 Campaign in San Francisco" (1986) at the Labor Archives and Research Center, 480 Winston Way, San Francisco. Also read Katharine Marino's article "Maud Younger and the San Francisco Wage Earner's Suffrage League: Standing Firmly for Working Class Women", *California Historian*, Fall, 1997.

The Shafroth amendment citation is in the *Congressional Record* for the 63rd Congress, 2nd Session, December 1, 1913, to October 24, 1914. For a detailed article about the 1915 cross-country roadster trip, highlighting Sara Bard Field's participation, read Amelia Fry's "Along the Suffrage Trail," *American History*, January, 1969. Also check newspaper accounts of that eventful sendoff, September 16, 1915.

All music sheets for "Buy A Broom" and "March of the Women" are from the San Francisco Main Library; the music department. For "March of the Women" and Sara Bard Field's words to the "Marsellaise," see the suffrage file on the sixth floor.

Sources: Illustrations and Images

All the archival art and images were photographed and resuscitated by Sue Cazaly.

Cover Image: from Ella Sterling Cummins' *Story of the Files*, 1894, author's copy;.

Page 4: Dedication page: from Selina Solomon's cover *How We Won the Vote in California*, San Francisco Main Library, History Center, 6th Floor.

Page 6: Acknowledgement page: from *Story of the Files*.

Page 7: "Women Vote" handout from suffrage files, San Francisco Main Library, History Center, 6th Floor.

Page 13: "Inspiration of the Suffrage Cause" image from *San Francisco Call-Bulletin*, Sept. 18, 1915.

Page 14: Laura de Force Gordon picture, Bank of Stockton archives.

Page 15: Georgianna Bruce Kirby from *Story of the Files*.

Page 16: "Champions of Woman Suffrage" *San Francisco Chronicle*, July 11, 1871.

Page 17: "Shall Women Vote?" *San Francisco Chronicle* editorial, July 11, 1871.

Page 18: Woman Suffrage poem, *San Francisco Chronicle*, February 4, 1870.

Page 20: Emily Pitts Stevens picture, the California Historical Society, San Francisco, CA.

Page 21: Masthead of *California Sunday Mercury*, the Bancroft Library, Berkeley, California.

Page 23: *Carrier Dove* cover, July 27, 1889, San Francisco Main Library, History Center, 6th Floor.

Page 24: Title page of *Astrea*, San Francisco Main Library, History Center, 6th Floor, two poems: "Ode" and "Labor is Worship."

Page 27: Women's Cooperative Printing Union ad in *West Coast Journal*, May 18, 1870, the Bancroft Library, Berkeley, California.

Page 28: Marietta Beers-Stow portrait from her 1876 book, *Probate Confiscation*, the Bancroft Library, Berkeley, California.

Page 29: Ellen Clark Sargent picture from Selina Solomons', *How We Won the Vote in California*, San Francisco Main Library, History Center, 6th Floor.

Page 31: 1895 California Woman's Congress Association Board and Staff picture, the California Historical Society, San Francisco, Mm. Sorbier's papers.

Page 32: "The Hand that Rocks the Cradle Rears the Patriot" newspaper image, the Bancroft Library, Berkeley, California, Ponds-McHenry-Keith papers.

Page 33: Sarah B. Cooper picture, San Francisco Main Library, History Center, 6th Floor.

Page 34: Fourth Star handout, the Bancroft Library, Berkeley, California, Ponds-McHenry-Keith papers.

Page 35: Bifurcated skirt image from the *San Francisco Call*, May 1892.

Page 36: Women's Place in the Home, *San Francisco Call*, September 18, 1915.

Page 37: Stars of Liberty, *San Francisco Examiner*, June 17, 1896

Page 38: "Will Leave Them No Chance to Escape," *San Francisco Examiner*, June 17, 1896.

Page 39: 1896 Campaign Team, the California Historical Society, S.F., CA.

Page 40: Mary McHenry Keith portrait, the Bancroft Library, Berkeley, California, Ponds-McHenry-Keith papers.

Page 41: Young Mary McHenry portrait, the Bancroft Library, Berkeley, California, Ponds-McHenry-Keith papers.

Page 42: Reception invitation card, the Bancroft Library, Berkeley, California, Hester Harland papers.

Page 43: Political Equality handout, Bancroft Library, Berkeley, California, Hester Harland papers.

Pgae 44: Clara Shortridge Foltz portrait, the Bancroft Library, Berkeley, California..

Page 45: Clara Shortridge Foltz portrait, the Bancroft Library, Berkeley, California..

Pgae 46: Jimmy Swinnerton cartoons from the *San Francisco Examiner*, November 4, 1896.

Page 47: Delegate badge to State Woman's Suffrage Convention, the Bancroft Library, Berkeley, California..

Page 49: *Western Women*, Bancroft Library, Berkeley, California, Ponds-McHenry-Keith papers.

Page 50-51: Program, October 24, 1902, Bancroft Library, Berkeley, California, Ponds-McHenry-Keith papers.

Page 52: NAWSA badge, Bancroft Library, Berkeley, California, Ponds-McHenry-Keith papers.

Page 53: Nellie Holbrook Blinn, Bancroft Library, Berkeley, California, suffrage files.

Page 54: August 27, 1908, Oakland March, the California Historical Society, San Francisco.

Page 55: Lillian Harris Coffin picture from Solomons', *How We Won in the Vote in California*, San Francisco Main Library, History Center, 6th Floor.

Page 57: Cover of *How We Won the Vote in California*, San Francisco Main Library, History Center, 6th Floor.

Page 58: Selena Solomons' portrait in her book *How We Won in the Vote in California*, San Francisco Main Library, History Center, 6th Floor.

Page 59: "Justice to California Women" handout, San Francisco Main Library, History Center, 6th Floor, suffrage files.

Page 60: "California Women Have No Votes" handout, Bancroft Library, Berkeley, California, suffrage files.

Page 61: "Votes for Women" prize-winning poster, Bancroft Library, Berkeley, California, Equal Suffrage League files.

Page 62-63: "Buy a Broom" sheet music from 3rd floor Main Library, San Francisco.

Page 64: "Another Star" by permission from the Bancroft Library, Berkeley, California, suffrage file.

Page 65: Elizabeth Lowe Watson picture in *How We Won in the Vote in California*, San Francisco Main Library, History Center, 6th Floor.

Page 66: Berkeley Suffrage Campaign Headquarters handout, the Bancroft Library, Berkeley, California, Hester Harland papers.

Page 67: "Votes for Women" handout, San Francisco Main Library, History Center, 6th Floor.

Page 68: "Women Should Vote" handout, the Bancroft Library, Berkeley, California, suffrage file.

Page 69: Minna O'Donnell picture from the *San Francisco Call*, August 19, 1911.

Page 70-71: "Why Wage-Earning Women Should Vote", San Francisco Main Library, History Center, 6th Floor.

Page 71: Maud Younger picture from the California State Library collection, Sacramento, California.

Page 72: "Voters for Mothers" handout, the Bancroft Library, Berkeley, California, suffrage file.

Page 73: "I Believe in the Food, if not the Vote" by Phil Rader in *San Francisco Bulletin*, March 26, 1910

Page 74: The *San Francisco Call* headline, August 6, 1911, the Bancroft Library, Berkeley, California, suffrage file.

Page 75: "Women Lead in Ballot" article in The *San Francisco Call*, October 12, 1911, the Bancroft Library, Berkeley, California, suffrage file.

Page 76: "Suffrage Auto Parade" article, *Berkeley Independent*, October 4, 1911, the Bancroft Library, Berkeley, California, suffrage file.

Page 77: "Out of the Dust" poem from College Equal Suffrage League files in the Bancroft Library, Berkeley, California.

Page 78: "Women Vote in San Francisco in 1912", California State Library Collection, Sacramento, California.

Page 79: "What? Back Again So Soon?" cartoon from the *San Francisco Call*, September 18, 1915.

Page 80: Shafroth Amendment (S 3507) in *San Francisco Call*, September 18, 1915.

Page 81: Full page cartoon, *San Francisco Call*, September 18, 1915.

Page 82: "Paper paper!", *San Francisco Call*, September 18, 1915.

Page 83: "Ballad of Suffragette," *San Francisco Call*, September 18, 1915.

Page 84: "And Without Representation," *San Francisco Call*, September 18, 1915.

Page 85: "Song of Free Women,", San Francisco Main Library, History Center, 6th Floor.

Page 86-87: Congressional Union for Woman Suffrage program (2 pages), San Francisco Main Library, History Center, 6th Floor, PPIE file.

Page 88: Alice Paul picture from Doris Stevens' *Jailed for Freedom*.

Page 89: Willys Overland ad, *San Francisco Call*, September 18, 1915.

Page 91: "Court of Abundance,", San Francisco Main Library, History Center, 6th Floor, PPIE file.

Page 92: "March of the Women", San Francisco Main Library, History Center, 6th Floor.

Page 93: Bear image from Cummins' *Story of the Files*.

Page 95: *San Francisco Sunday Call*, July 4, 1909, Bancroft Library, Berkeley, California, suffrage files.

Men come and men go, but a truth goes marching on

In a true DEMOCRACY every citizen has a vote.

We are half the human race.
—Charlotte Perkins Gilman

We shall never have equal rights until we have taken them, nor respect until we command it. Act up to your convictions of justice and right, and you cannot go far wrong.
—Belva A. Lockwood

Women's suffrage is not a struggle in which men are to be the losers and women the gainers. It is a struggle in which both are to gain and lose alike. —Emily Pitts-Stevens

THE HAND THAT ROCKS THE CRADLE REARS THE PATRIOT.

One-seventh of the taxes in California are paid by women, and it is only natural that they should wish to have some voice in the matter of the expenditure of money.
—Susan B. Anthony

Liberty is the fundamental desire of the human spirit.

In a true democracy every citizen has a vote. No self-respecting woman should work for the success of a party that ignores her sex.
—Susan B. Anthony

No nation can rise higher than its women.

Mae Kramer Silver

Mae Kramer Silver came to San Francisco from New Jersey in 1960. She holds a B.S. triple major in Education, History and English from Trenton State College (1955), and a M.S.W. from Rutgers University (1958). After a career as a Licensed Clinical Social Worker, Mae became a history writer and an independent scholar focusing on San Francisco neighborhood history. She particularly enjoys those stories no one else has written—such as *The Sixth Star*. In addition to writing history, Mae served as a founding director of the San Francisco Historical Society and as secretary, vice president and president of the San Francisco History Association. Currently she is a member of the Women's History committee of The Women's Building.

Writing since 1984, Mae has published numerous articles in *Western States Jewish Historical Journal*, *Argonaut*, *Friends of the Library News*, *San Francisco Officer's News*, *Hastings Community* and *Westerners Vignettes*, as well as local neighborhood papers. She won a history writing prize in the San Francisco County Fair in 1984.

Abraham Lincoln said: Women Should Vote. What do you say?

No taxation without representation.

Democracy should begin at home.

With Justice and Liberty for all.

Forward out of Error, Forward into Light.

Resistance to tyranny is obedience to God.

Leave behind the night.

Give your girl the same chance as your boy.

Let women help. Two heads are better than one.

Justice demands the vote.

How long must women wait for liberty?

Women should be armed with the ballot.

Sue Cazaly

A native born Californian from Delano, Sue Cazaly received her B.A. in Education and Art from San Jose State University (1955) and an M.A. in Art and photography from Ohio State University (1972). Her specialized outdoors photography has been published in *Persimmon Hill* magazine, *California Art Review*, *Grassland Review* (University of North Texas), *New Poetry Journal*, *The Spirit That Moves Us* Press, *Poet's Market Book* and *Journal of the West*. She has exhibited at the Bay Window Gallery, in Mendocino; Mendocino Art Center; Phoenix Art Museum, in Phoenix, Arizona; Gallery F22, in Santa Fe, New Mexico; Morro Bay Natural History Museum, Juried Photo Salon, in Daly City, California; and the Shasta County Art Council, in Redding, California. Sue has served as chairperson of the Display Committee of the historic San

Francisco Women Artists Gallery since 1992. Slide Shows and Documentation: The Nature Conservancy—Carrizo Plain, Smithsonian—Carrizo Plain, University of California, Mono Lake, *19th Century San Francisco Women Artists* with Mae Silver, *The Sixth Star* with Mae Silver.

Chris Carlsson

As the designer of *The Sixth Star*, Chris Carlsson combines fascination for forgotten history with his graphic art talents and political sensibilities. He is a prolific writer and artist who has lately produced the award-winning *Shaping San Francisco*, which honors forgotten and neglected local history on computer kiosks installed in several public locations throughout the city. He also co-edited *Reclaiming San Francisco: History, Politics, Culture* (City Lights, 1998). In July, 1999, the *San Francisco Bay Guardian* named Chris a "Local Hero" for his work about the city's forgotten histories. As co-owner of Typesetting, Etc., Chris provides a crucial link between creators and printers. He is the indispensable in-between spirit in *The Sixth Star*.

Index